MW01297664

JUL 2 2 2013

D R Toi
PO Box 1698
Newport News, VA 23601

Nov. 23-2013-

光

THE PRANA PROGRAM

with Jasmuheen

For the children of our world.
May we all obtain the nourishment that we need
as we explore the micro-food of life.

~S.E.A.~

Self Empowerment Academy

P.O. Box 1754, Buderim, QLD, Australia

Fax: +61 7 5445 6075

www.selfempowermentacademy.com.au

www.jasmuheen.com

Draft edition released October 2005
Published January 2006

The Prana Program with Jasmuheen
ISBN 978-1-84728-343-6

e-book produced January 2006

Please respect the work of the author
& help S.E.A. promote planetary peace.

For more copies go to
http://www.selfempowermentacademy.com.au/htm/cia-education.asp#pranaprogram

THE PRANA PROGRAM
Enjoyable & Effective Evolution

**Everything
you need
to know
about
prana**

**Understanding the new Micro-food
Alternate Energy for the New Millennium
Common Questions & Simple Conversions
Including Prana Program for Third World
Countries & World Health & Hunger Issues**

Introduction

As I travel the world again this year I can feel how the fields are changing in response to the ever expanding consciousness among humanity on Earth. Each day I get guidance to write and to focus on simplifying the Prana Divine Nutrition agenda by doing a basic question and answer style book.

Although some of this has been covered in the Divine Nutrition Trilogy, there always seems to be new information to add and new, simpler perspectives to hold. I also find that as time progresses and my own consciousness expands, that I understand things at deeper levels, particularly as I keep exploring my own potential and following my inner guidance. Also as we are now 12 years on from our initial experiential research, this reality has now been firmly anchored in the morphogenetic field, allowing the pathway and the access program to be more powerful and easily utilized, especially with our understanding now driven more by field science than just by esoteric principles of love, faith and trust.

The title "Enjoyable & Effective Evolution" flows into my mind as I recognize again the bigger perspective of the prana game and how it can change humanity's future, for the more we increase the pranic flow through our bodies, the healthier and happier we become. We also enhance our ability to find perfect resolutions to many of our world's challenges.

Aware of my upcoming meeting at the end of this year with a group of people in Vienna who are pro-active with Third World aid programs, I realize also that it is time for me to download from the Universal Field of Infinite Love and Intelligence a more practical program for prana as nourishment into Third World countries. Thankfully as time has progressed and more of us in the west choose to be nourished in this way, our path has become easier to share and the tools easier to apply. After watching a BBC documentary on poverty and death via malnutrition and starvation in Ethiopia, an inner voice tells me it is time to apply all our research into a simpler, pragmatic program and to use my political connections to implement it globally where needed.

Some may say that people in these countries choose to be born into these circumstances for their own karmic learning and while this is true for us all, that does not mean that basic human rights need to be ignored while we complete our personal evolutionary path. Part of humanity enjoying a more effective evolution is our learning to unify and distribute resources – physical, emotional, mental and spiritual – in a more supportive and compassionate manner.

Sharing our understanding of the power of prana will help to facilitate this.

Also it is not just Third World countries who need the education of The Prana Program for as we shared in the book *The Food of Gods*, everyone is hungry for something whether it be love, health, wealth, passion, purpose, personal and planetary peace or even enlightenment. In these desires humanity is the same, yet our western education system rarely teaches us how to effectively, harmoniously and permanently satisfy all of our hungers. Throughout the last four decades of my experiential metaphysical research I have only found one way to satisfy all human hunger and that is by increasing the levels of prana that we can attract, hold and then radiate through ourselves and then into the world. With this has come the most amazing cache of unexpected gifts particularly as I understand more about the micro-food flow of life.

As I look back over the past decade and what we have achieved with the Prana Program and why I first went public, I realize that it was always for the children. The idea that children were dying unnecessarily from hunger related diseases has irritated me since I was a child, as it seemed so fixable, given the resources that we have in our world. These days my attitude is that if we can't rely on governments to address this more successfully, then we can rely on human resources and education at a grass-roots level instead, education that allows us access to alternate methods to address this – such as The Prana Program. Perhaps it was this early childhood irritation that has given me the stamina to continue to play this game. In his book *The Present* author Spencer Johnson encourages us to not just learn from the past, but to enjoy and be focused in the present, and to plan for the future, if we want it to be brighter than today, and this is what The Prana Program is about – creating a brighter future just because we can.

Over the past decade I have heard and answered so many questions regarding The Prana Program that in this book we will attempt to share them all, catergorizing them into specific areas of interest and also hopefully dispelling some of the rumors that have arisen over the years about the path through which I personally discovered the nourishing power of prana.

We also include how to use The Prana Program effectively in Third World countries as well as the personal benefits of doing so in our own lives no matter where we live. While our focus is primarily on answering commonly asked questions, unlike our other research manuals this is not an e-book that will provide indepth "how to's". Nonetheless in the final section for Third World countries I will attempt to offer the simplest "how to" program that I now know. We trust you will enjoy our findings, any repetition of answers occurs simply to elaborate on a point or to add a different or more expanded perspective.   Namaste Jasmuheen

Contents

1. Enjoyable & Effective Evolution — 13
   - Evolution, Ascension & Enlightenment — 17

2. Identification, Benefits & Insights
   - Identification — 23
   - Prana Program Benefits — 28
   - Prana & The Bio-system — 29
   - Prana & Our DOW — 33
   - Prana & The Heart — 34
   - Prana & Emotional, Mental & Spiritual Food — 37
   - Prana & The Brain — 40
   - Prana & Darkroom Technology — 43
   - Prana & The Cells — 44
   - Prana & Field Science — 47
   - Prana & Inter-dimensional Life — 55

3. Preparation, Physical Changes & Pre-programming — 58

4. Calibration, Testing & Comfortable Conversions — 77

5. Social Scenes
   - Prana & Social Behaviour — 96
   - Prana & Parenting — 100
   - Prana & Other Family Members – Harmonizing Households — 102
   - Prana & Eating Disorders — 104
   - Prana, Sexuality & Our Romantic Relationships — 105

6. Global Issues – Gifts & Growth
   - Past, Present & Future — 108

	Prana & Health	113
	Prana & Religion	115
	The Prana Program & The Environment	118
	The Prana Program & Politics	119
7.	Q & A's on the 21 day Process, Skeptics & The Media	123
8.	Solar Nourishment, Bigu & The Bigger Picture	134
9.	Prana Program for Third World Challenges	141
	Intentions & Outcomes	144
	a) Mental Attitudes & Mindsets	146
	b) Community Life & Supportive Fields	152
	c) Alternate Pragmatic Internal Feeding Mechanisms	157
	d) A simple Solar Feeding Program & Bigu & Research	169
	e) Resource Sustainability & Environmental Statistics	174
	f) Resource Redistribution & The Prana Program	177

Index	183
Jasmuheen's Background	193
Other relevant e-books with Jasmuheen	197

THE PRANA PROGRAM

WHAT: The Prana Program is designed to re-harmonize the world and eliminate all health and hunger challenges.

WHY: Because we have the knowledge how and can do it to create a more effective and enjoyable evolution.

WHERE: All countries – with the program tailor made to focus on Third World countries. Overall goal – elimination of all health and hunger challenges in ALL countries.

HOW: The Prana Program as a holistic educational tool utilizing political, media and grass-roots networks.

WHEN: Beginning now and continuing until the goal is achieved.

OUTCOME: Global unity, harmony, health and peace as we nourish ourselves more from the micro-food flow of life.

ॐ 1 ॐ

Enjoyable & Effective Evolution

Definition of evolution from: ***http://www.wordiq.com/definition/Evolution***

Evolution generally refers to any process of change over time. In the context of life science, evolution is a change in the genetic makeup of a population of interbreeding individuals within a species. Since the emergence of modern genetics in the 1940's, evolution has been defined more specifically as a change in the frequency of alleles from one generation to the next. (An allele is any one of a number of alternative forms of the same gene occupying a given locus (position) on a chromosome.)

Q: What do you define as an enjoyable and effective evolution?
A: To evolve in a way that is effective means an evolutionary process where we live in harmony with all kingdoms – animal, plant and human and even mineral, without destroying the natural balance of resources. This occurs when we understand that every being is part of a whole and that everyone's existence thus impacts upon our path because we are all interconnected. For example, collectively to ignore the poor and the suffering, and our ability to provide basic human rights, globally limits the enjoyment of our evolution for 2/3's of our population. When we recognize this interconnectedness and work as a harmonious whole then we will have an effective and also more enjoyable evolutionary path as the ability to work in harmony is a sign of a civilized world.

Individually an effective and enjoyable evolution can be measured by our personal levels of health and happiness which is a reflection of our physical, emotional, mental and spiritual wellbeing.

Q: There appears to be so much suffering in our world today, how can The Prana Program change this so that we have a more enjoyable and effective evolution, individually and as a species?
A: Through education we can inspire people to increase the pranic flow through their beings which then changes their personal resonance and how the universe responds to them. The Prana Program path is about mastering energy flow within us and around us so that we can consciously create a present and a future that provides increased health and happiness levels for all.

Q: What is prana?
A: Called the microfood of life, according to http://www.wordiq.com/dictionary.html, "prana is the vital air, or breath, of the human body, as visualized in Hinduism. It is also interpreted as the vital,

life-sustaining force of both the individual body and the universe. Its first expounding came in the Upanishads, where it is part of the worldly, physical realm, sustaining the body and reliant on the mind. Prana suffuses all living form but is not itself the soul."

Q: What exactly is pranic nourishment and how does it work, where and when did it originate?

A: The idea of prana as nourishment has been around since the dawn of time. Universal Mind and its Akashic records, share that there was a time where all beings were sustained from the pranic forces. Pranic nourishment is the ability to attract and then absorb all the nutrients, vitamins and nourishment one requires, to maintain a healthy being, from the universal life force a force which is also termed cosmic particles or chi energy.

A person who practices this does not need to take their nourishment from physical food and they also find that by increasing the pranic flow through their bodies they are fed not just physically but also emotionally, mentally and spiritually due to the nature of the pranic flow. Being fed in this way allows us a more effective and enjoyable evolution for reasons we will cover throughout *The Prana Program* book.

Q: In the west we have now begun to recognize prana as an alternate food source for the physical body, how can it feed us on other levels?

A: When we increase the flow of pure prana within us its presence and essence floods through the system and transforms limiting aspects of how the human biological system is operating thus allowing an individual to access and demonstrate natural but generally dormant abilities. The activation of these abilities provides us with emotional, mental and spiritual nourishment.

Q: What exactly are some of these 'natural but dormant abilities'?

A: The human system is a complex one and currently we use limited sections of our brain as that is all that is required to survive here. Metaphysics can teach us how to access our natural clairvoyant, clairaudient and clairsentient abilities and how to utilize other sections of our brain which according to the science of neuro-theology is hardwired to deliver a variety of experiences that may appear to be supernatural but are actually natural when a person expands their consciousness and anchors their brainwaves into different patterns of behavior.

Q: Why will the activation of these abilities make human evolution more effective and enjoyable?

A: Activation of these abilities will produce a more loving, compassionate and aware species who will operate en mass for the good of the whole and who will be less driven by limited ego perspectives and paradigms of greed and power. Currently 95% of our planetary resources are controlled by 5% of our population with approximately one half of our population living on less than two US dollars per day, in very limited conditions with limited access to healthy food, decent shelter or education programs that can teach them how to break cycles of poverty. There comes a point in the evolution of every species where these issues need to be resolved effectively and harmoniously and this process is just a natural part of human refinement.

Q: Does a person need to be a metaphysician to work with or utilize the pranic force more effectively for the evolutionary process?

A: No but we need to know how to create a mental model of reality that allows us to recognize, be open to, and consciously work with, the pranic flow. This happens more powerfully and easily when we understand universal laws as the higher laws behind creation, particularly the Law of Resonance that says like attracts like. Metaphysics is simply the understanding of the science of life. We also need effective, pragmatic and simple tools to harmonize our internal and external energy flow which then delivers many personal and global benefits.

Q: Why is increasing the pranic flow within us an answer to a more effective evolution?

A: Basically it stimulates the release of higher intelligence within us. Prana is composed of various aspects some of which are the invisible mathematical codes that drive and operate matter in form and all of creation. As we increase the influx of this pranic flow within us, it stimulates the same dormant mathematical codes within us to awaken, thus providing us with clearer and greater insights as to the purpose of our existence and the choices we have as creator beings. Increasing its flow within us allows us to perceive life from a different perspective as it expands our awareness and activates the usage of our master glands – the pituitary and pineal – and stimulates them to function in a different way. These glands also regulate our brain wave patterns to either Beta, Alpha, Theta or Delta wave frequencies.

Q: Are brain wave patterns connected to the creation of a more positive human evolutionary cycle?

A: Most definitely. Research has already established that holding Alpha brain wave patterns makes us less stressed and consequently healthier and that this is achieved through the practice of things like yoga, meditation and positive thinking. Our research has found that when we can stabilize our brain wave patterns into the Theta zones then this also magnetizes more prana to us and gives us much more freedom from perceived human limitations.

Q: If prana provides the building blocks of all life, then doesn't everyone live on prana already?
A: Yes, but in the west we have not been educated into appreciating all its attributes and the benefits that we can experience when we consciously increase its flow within us.

Q: What exactly has prana to do with a more enjoyable evolution?
A: Firstly, the better informed we are as to our true nature the happier we are. Our true essence or nature is a pool of pure prana that has the ability to remain unpolluted by mind/ego/cultural conditioning although it can be diluted in strength and its physical expression by these things.

Prana is also the only form of nourishment that can feed us on all levels as it goes beyond our religious and cultural concepts. It is our common human bond and increasing its flow eliminates feelings of separation, loneliness, frustration, fear and ignorance thus making life more enjoyable.

Prana can actually be felt as an inner pulsation of love so increasing its flow increases our experience of self love and love for others. Pranic energy can be utilized for self healing, transmutation, improving our intuitive abilities and increasing the pranic flow internally and externally helps us to eliminate all physical, emotional, mental and spiritual toxicity and pollution. The less diluted the pranic flow is, the more magic, wonder, synchronicity and Grace we experience in our daily life.

Q: You talk a lot about increasing and sometimes even purifying the pranic flow through a body to gain certain individual and global benefits and to positively influence the course of human evolution, what exactly do you mean by this?
A: Prana is the base frequency of all cells as it gives life to all molecules and atomic structure, however as our cells store mental and emotional imprints from our experiences in life, sometimes cells can be polluted with emotional and mental toxicity, to the point that the pranic flow is diluted. This results in unhappiness and/or disease within a system and eventually the system breaks down and dies. By consciously increasing the pranic flow, because it is a pure energy with transmuting powers, we can recalibrate our cells back into a more supportive frequency that enhances both the quality and quantity of our life.

Q: Why would a person want to increase the pranic flow in their body?

A: The benefits of doing this – when understood – make it a very attractive way to exist in this world and makes our personal and global evolutionary process not only more effective but also more enjoyable. Briefly as mentioned some of these benefits are the elimination of all disease on physical, emotional, mental and spiritual levels, the unification of our species into a more harmonious and respectful state of coexistence and the elimination of all pollution on our planet.

EVOLUTION, ASCENSION & ENLIGHTENMENT

Q: Some may say that in order to experience a more effective and enjoyable evolution we all need to become a little more enlightened. Is this something The Prana Program attends to?

A: Most definitely, one definition of enlightenment is being filled with light. Light has natural aspects of love and wisdom. To be enlightened is to be aware of and demonstrate these aspects of our true nature. By consciously flooding our system with pure prana we can – as mentioned – activate aspects of our nature that are able to guide us to make wise and loving choices which is a sign of being filled with light.

It is important to note that on one level there is no such thing as enlightenment for we can always increase our capacity to handle more light therefore being enlightened is not a destination but a continual journey.

Q: According to your first book on The Prana Program **Pranic Nourishment – Nutrition for the New Millennium** *(also known as* **Living on Light***) your own initial attraction to The Prana Program was an interest in ascension, can you comment on this?*

A: Although I am often known as the person who is a proponent of pranic nourishment and its gift of no longer having to take physical food, initially this in itself was of little interest to me although I was very aware of the relevance of this aspect of The Prana Program to world health and world hunger issues. Nonetheless at that point in my life – the early 1990's – I was more interested in increasing my inner light quotient for the experience of love and wisdom that this would bring. My driving motivation was to be the best version of a human being that I could be which meant being a person who experienced and radiated love and wisdom. The fact that when we increase our radiation levels of this love flow, that it can feed us physically, was to me a small and relatively inconsequential bonus.

Q: Can you say something about Ascension?

A: Ascension is not something that I focus on anymore as we are made perfect in the image of the Creator – we've just forgotten how to act like we are. As we are fulfilling a service agenda blueprint, our current focus is on more practical things like are we all happy and healthy, do we have a lot of love in our life and does the way each of us live enhance the planet or does it perpetuate separation and chaos?

Our focus for many years has been on lifestyle tools – things to do to get emotionally, mentally, physically and spiritually fit. When we're fit on all levels we exist in a personal paradise and global paradise flows naturally in from that. Ascension and enlightenment are just one aspect of the package and to experience these things practically we need to be tuned perfectly to the channel of the Divine One Within – our DOW – who loves us enough to gift us with the breath of life.

Q: You talk about 'we' a lot in your answers. What do you mean by 'we'?

A: 'We' are the beings of light and love that I work with on the internal and external planes. Souls committed to the positive expansion of consciousness on Earth and the sharing of The Prana Program benefits.

Q: There is talk in metaphysical circles that humanity is at a crossroad and can choose a path of enjoyable evolution, through reawakening to their true nature and experiencing its gifts, or a path of continual chaos which some metaphysicians say comes from ignoring our true nature. Can you comment on this and why The Prana Program is relevant to this choice?

A: Holistic Education is education in understanding the way a human bio-system operates as a whole – as a physical, emotional, mental and spiritual being. In order to make wise choices we need to be well informed as to human potential and capability. We have seen the outcome of just working from limited mental plane perspectives without utilizing our higher, more refined intuitive nature and how this has resulted in a world living in fear, with terrorism and war being a regular occurrence for many.

The world has long seen the division that comes when we try to address the spiritual aspect of our being as religious doctrine often promotes separation, so in many circles religion and politics are rarely discussed due to the divisive nature of the topics and also because many believe that religious beliefs are personal and sacred. Nonetheless we cannot continue to ignore holistic education so we need to find a way to address spirituality and to do this independently of religion, or without challenging the sanctity of people's sacred beliefs.

For many the best way to do this has been through metaphysics where we study the science of spirituality and life and learn experientially about resonance and energy fields. Increasing the pranic flow is simply a way of redirecting internal and external energy to set up a different reaction from, and within, the universal field. When we decrease or dilute the pranic flow we experience disease and chaos, when we increase the flow we experience harmony, health, peace and fulfillment.

Q: Although you will discuss many of The Prana Program benefits during your 2006 world tour and throughout* The Prana Program *e-book, what is the greatest gift The Prana Program can give our evolving species?
A: Personally I think the greatest gift that The Prana Program can give us is a clear pathway and the energy support to create a peaceful and harmonious world and to do it with minimal effort, by using the energy of Grace, as it can boost our EQ – our emotional intelligence quotient.

Q: Can you explain Grace further?
A: Grace is an energy that is regulated by the pranic flow. The more intense or pure the pranic flow and the less we dilute it with physical, emotional and mental toxicity, the more Grace we magnetize to our energy field. Grace brings miracles, magic, synchronicity and minimum effort to our existence as it acts like a wave that allows us to surf through the fields of life with ease and joy and a feeling of just rightness. According to the Oxford dictionary Grace is the unmerited favor of God, a divinely regenerating, inspiring, and strengthening influence.

Q: The Indian yogis say that Grace cannot be captured and it comes to those when it is ready. What have you found?
A: While this is true in essence, a human being can tune themselves – via their lifestyle choice – to the same field of resonance as Grace, which is like putting ourselves on a cosmic freeway where Grace flows so that sooner or later we get picked up by its current. One thing our experiential research has also found is that as soon as a person's focus shifts from the sole preoccupation of "I" to the "we" paradigm, in that they are more compassionate and aware of how their behavior impacts upon the whole – and so they set their intention to act in a way that is beneficial to the world – then they automatically attract more Grace to their field.

Q: At what stage of evolution are the people who come to hear of your research?

A: I tend to classify them into four stages.

The first group are basically just curious and some of these are also highly skeptical.

The second are at the stage of beginning to remember they are more than just mind and body so they are open to the path of self refinement and are seeking to experience their DOW, the one that breathes them, as intuitively they feel it has the key to improving their happiness and/or health levels. These ones often desire to experience more Grace and synchronicity and so are beginning to expand their sense of intuition and higher knowing.

The third group are experiencing a lot of happiness, much better health and are generally more focused on the service agenda and having their presence make a positive difference in the world. Through meditation they are often exploring the inner planes and generally expanding their consciousness to understand their potential. Their experience of Grace and synchronicity is a lot more regular and they are usually hungry for consistency of this. In this state many start to work inter-dimensionally where some may come into contact with the Angelic realms and the Holy Ones.

The fourth group are healthy and happy as they have witnessed of lot of synchronicity and magic in their life and, feeling complete, are now focused only on service. You could say that they have graduated and so they are no longer being overshadowed by the Holy Ones to the degree of group one and two. In this state they often have no more questions, they understand the power of radiation, are generally at one with their DOW, and enjoy the state of Being rather than doing. In my experience it is usually groups three and four who can comprehend more fully the reality that nourishment can come from other 'invisible' sources such as prana or Divine Love.

Q: Are people who choose to live only on a pure prana diet enlightened or special?
A: Not necessarily. It is important to note that our capacity to attract hold and radiate more love, light and wisdom is constantly expanding and the more we expand into displaying these attributes, the more gifts we receive from them. Remember like attracts like, so the more we radiate the love and wisdom of our divine nature, the more we attract love and wisdom to us from the universal field which acts as a mirror of our own consciousness. To attract enough prana to be successfully nourished and free from the need of physical food does require us to live a certain lifestyle to attract more cosmic particles, so perhaps we are 'special' in how we choose to spend our time.

Q: Is it true that an individual must have attained a certain level in their own personal evolution to even be interested in the idea of prana as a form of alternate nourishment?

A: On one level yes. If we see planet Earth as a school of limitation and accept that individuals as systems of energy constantly change form via the process of reincarnation, then it can often take many lifetimes until the idea of being limited and moving beyond this ceases to fascinate an evolving soul. It is said that many souls come to Earth expressly to experience its density and limitation, to know the joys of having five senses and the fun of eating, drinking water or wine, the joy of sex and procreation and all that Earth offers as we clothe ourselves in physical matter.

However, there also comes a time in a soul's evolution here that their two higher senses of intuition and knowing become more active so that we soon long to move beyond duality and feelings of separation and merge back into an experience of being part of a more unified whole. The drive to be harmoniously integrated with all aspects of our being – from lower to higher levels – comes to all souls in time once they have learnt most of what being on the Earth plane has to teach them.

Consciously rebalancing karmic ties, fulfilling personal blueprints and global service agendas then become more of a focus as does the idea of positively contributing to Earth's evolutionary process. With this type of drive we find ourselves more open to experiencing the gifts of our higher, more divine essence nature, one of which is its ability to nourish us and free us from the need to take our sustenance from the physical world. All of this is part of our natural evolutionary cycle as eternal spiritual beings having a temporary human experience.

Q: What do you say to people who say, just be in the moment, relax, life is perfect as it is, why try to change the world?

A: This is a valid insight for someone who is seeking, or exploring, the Theta or Delta brain wave pattern realms, however we are in this world to give and to receive. What we can share is our experiential research with holistic education – an educational paradigm that keeps evolving as we do. This is a way of being which can refine our world so that everyone gets to see the beauty of life and move into the state of experience where they feel that every moment is perfect. While it's easier to relax in the west as our basic needs are taken care of, for people struggling to survive it is a different game and one we can all make less difficult with a bit of compassion and insight.

Each being is a cell in the body of a Divinely Perfect Being, but as in the human system, some cells can be infected with a virus of disharmony. When this happens, the body as a whole works together to bring everything into perfect health and balance.

It is true that you can bring your personal resonance into such a state of alignment with your Divine Essence that the universe rolls in ecstasy at your feet. The Austrian philosopher and poet Franz Kafka once said: "You need not leave your room. Remain sitting at your table and listen. You need not even listen, simply wait. You need not even wait, just learn to become quite, and still, and solitary. The world will freely offer itself to you to be unmasked. It has no choice; it will roll in ecstasy at your feet." In this state you do nothing as all unfolds perfectly around you and for you but all of this is dependant on our personal resonance which we can all alter at will.

☙ 2 ❧

Identification, Benefits & Insights

IDENTIFICATION

Q: What is a bio-system?
A: The term bio-system in this context refers to the human biological system.

Q: What is a four body system and why is it necessary to tune and integrate the bio-system in order to experience the benefits of The Prana Program?
A: Research shares that human beings have a four body system – physical, emotional, mental and spiritual, that can be likened to a four string guitar. Each has their own note and when tuned, the music played (and the life lived) is magical and a being becomes both harmonized and limitless. When out of tune, people – like an 'out of tune' instrument – can experience various forms of emotional, physical or mental dis-ease. When these bodies are harmonized and integrated to support a common goal – such as the conscious manifestation and experience of our Divine essence through all realms, then The Prana Program is activated to another more potent level.

Q: What do you mean by Four Body Fitness?
A: Many metaphysicians are now convinced that personal health and happiness requires holistic education that also stimulates the activation of the seven senses. These include sight, sound, touch, taste, smell, intuition and the seventh sense of knowing, that sense that says, "I know that I know but I'm not sure what it is that I know but I know that I know it!" After decades of personal experimentation I have discovered that the sixth and seventh senses, and all our senses, can be refined and fully activated by our lifestyle choice.

I call the full activation of all our senses "Four Body Fitness" as this activation brings physical, emotional, mental and spiritual health and full activation of our senses can only occur when we are well tuned on all levels. Four Body Fitness allows us to have love, health, wealth, passion and purpose in life and also positive relationships with family and friends. It is also a sign of good pranic flow.

Q: In chapter one you defined what prana is, where can we get prana from?

A: We can attract more prana from internal and/or external planes. For example according to Master Choa Kok Sui – the founder of the 'Pranic Healing Network':

"Prana or ki is that life energy which keeps the body alive and healthy. In Greek it is called *pnuema*, in Polynesian *mana*, and in Hebrew *ruah*, which means "breath of life" …

"Basically, there are three major sources of prana: Solar prana, air prana, and ground prana. Solar prana is prana from sunlight. It invigorates the whole body and promotes good health. It can be obtained by sunbathing or exposure to sunlight for about five to ten minutes and by drinking water that has been exposed to sunlight. Prolonged exposure or too much solar prana would harm the whole physical body since it is quite potent.

"Prana contained in the air is called air prana or air vitality globule. Air prana is absorbed by the lungs through breathing and is also absorbed directly by the energy centers of the bioplasmic body. These energy centers are called chakras. More air prana can be absorbed by deep slow rhythmic breathing than by short shallow breathing. It can be also absorbed through the pores of the skin by persons who have undergone certain training.

"Prana contained in the ground is called ground prana or ground vitality globule. This is absorbed through the soles of the feet. This is done automatically and unconsciously. Walking barefoot increases the amount of ground prana absorbed by the body. One can consciously draw in more ground prana to increase one's vitality, capacity to do more work, and ability to think more clearly.

"Water absorbs prana from sunlight, air, and ground that it comes in contact with. Plants and trees absorb prana from sunlight, air, water, and ground. Men and animals obtain prana from sunlight, air, ground, water, and food. Fresh food contains more prana than preserved food."

There is also a way to draw prana inter-dimensionally via the atoms using alternate internal feeding mechanisms as shared in the last section of this book.

Q: Why is prana now being used as an alternative food source?

A: The rediscovery of this ancient yogic practice and the holistic education of its benefits in the west, will allow the western world – as a force of monetary power and compassionate conscience – to utilize this energy (along with aid and resource redistribution programs) to eliminate individual and global physical, emotional, mental and spiritual anorexia which I feel is currently responsible for most of the disharmony on Earth.

Metaphysically it is known that when a species is ready to take another positive step in their evolutionary journey, individuals who are tuned and open, are able to access, from the U.F.I. – the universal field of infinite love and intelligence – any data they need to achieve this so The Prana Program is now being experienced by more and more.

Q: Does a person need to have a good intellectual understanding of prana in order to experience its benefits?

A: Not at all. There are many people who calibrate naturally at the perfect levels to experience many of the benefits of The Prana Program. That said, education and information can be very beneficial. For example, I recently discovered that my new computer can do things that I was previously unaware of until my daughter told and showed me. These happen to be very beneficial features that I can now use that I previously didn't know of. Similarly with The Prana Program. Until we know what a system is capable of we cannot, and will not, unhook from older and often more limiting, habitual ways. Education widens our freedom of choice and can stimulate more creative thinking to fine tune our manifestation abilities.

Q: In your book The Food of Gods you talk about a three level system of Divine Nutrition. Can you explain this?

A: Briefly these are:-
- ☺ Level 1 is the gift of life – the fact that there is a force that loves us enough to constantly, automatically breathe life into us.
- ☺ Level 2 is being conscious of this force and using it to create physical, emotional, mental and spiritual fitness and to increase our health and happiness levels.
- ☺ Level 3 is exploring and accepting all the gifts this force can deliver when we increase its flow – particularly the gifts of freedom from perceived human limitations.

Q: So the Food of Gods is prana, is this also Elan Vital?

A: Yes, it is also called manna or food from heaven. It is produced in the body naturally and more can be attracted to the body via the internal and external planes. Another name for prana or Chi, Elan Vital is known as the force that brings inanimate objects to life. [n] (biology) a hypothetical force (not physical or chemical) once thought by Henri Bergson to cause the evolution and development of organisms.

Q: Is this force that you call prana the same as chi?

A: Yes, according to http://www.wordiq.com/dictionary.html, "Chi in English is often spelled as chi or ch'i. The Japanese form is ki. Qi is a fundamental concept of everyday Chinese culture, most often defined as "air" or "breath" (for example, the colloquial Mandarin Chinese term for "weather" is tiān qi, or the "breath of heaven") and, by extension, "life force" or "spiritual energy" that is part of everything that exists. References to qi or similar philosophical concepts as a type of metaphysical energy that sustains living beings are used in many belief systems, especially in Asia." Some of the Taosits masters also see chi as cosmic particles and say that where mind goes chi flows, so we need to understand the power of the mind in order to effectively influence energy dynamics and field flow.

Q: Is chi force then also a perfect blend of yin/yang energies and is that why The Prana Program requires internal energy balance?
A: Yes to both questions. According to Karen L. Scheel at:
http://www.almaranea.net/light/beginning.html: "To understand Chi we must look back to the very beginnings of Oriental Medicine to Taoism (pronounced: dow-ism) which means The Way. Taoism is the most influential root of Oriental Medicine. The ancient medicine people or Taoist's main focus was to observe the ways of the natural laws governing the universe as a method to understand the unseen inner world of our bodies.

"One of the philosophical foundations upon which their medical theories was built recognized that everything in the universe is composed of two complementary yet opposing energetic forces known as Yin (female) and Yang (male). Yin the female principle is associated with water and represents the Earth. Yang the male principle is associated with fire and represents heaven. Yin and Yang, female with male uniting the water energy of Earth along with the fire energy of heaven are the two primary forces that are responsible for all of creation. Together this energetic life force of Yin and Yang is known as Chi and means Energy."

Q: How does this chi flow through the body?
A: Again Karen L. Scheel writes: "The human body as a miniature universe houses 12 energetic channels or pathways wherein Chi flows. These channels are known as meridians and control both our gross and subtle anatomy. Our gross anatomy is the form that we can see whereas our subtle anatomy can not be seen by most individuals. This subtle energetic body represents the whole of who we are – our body, mind, emotions, and spirit. Unlike the veins that our blood flows through, meridian pathways also travel throughout the entire body but rather than as fluid for they deal more with energy and states of consciousness. Each meridian is associated with one of the Five Elements, each connects to a Yin or Yang organ of the body and they link our states of consciousness."

Q: Is prana the same as photon energy?

A: In The Prana Program context, many see the photon as forming an energy band of pure cosmic Christed consciousness, or pure Divine Love consciousness, that is currently bombarding the Earth to activate within her inhabitants a dormant force of love and wisdom that we need to use to make positive evolutionary choices. In this context prana and photons exhibit the same qualities.

On a science level, according to http://www.wordiq.com/dictionary.html, "In physics, the photon (from Greek φοτος, meaning light) is a quantum of excitation of the quantised electromagnetic field and is one of the elementary particles studied by quantum electrodynamics (QED) which is the oldest part of the Standard Model of particle physics. In layman's terms, photons are the building blocks of electromagnetic radiation: that is, a photon is a "particle" of light, although, according to quantum mechanics, all particles, including the photon, also have some of the properties of a wave."

Q: What about orgone energy?

A: At http://www.orgone.org/aaintro00.htm Charles R. Kelley wrote: "Franz Anton Mesmer called it animal magnetism; Charles von Reichenbach called it odyle. To Henri Bergson it was the elan vital, the "vital force"; while to Hans Driesch it was the entelechy. Sigmund Freud observed its functioning in human emotions and termed it libido. William MacDougall, the great British – American psychologist of a generation ago, labeled it hormic energy. Dozens, if not hundreds, of lesser – known scientists have recognized its presence and have given it a name to characterize its special properties. Among the 20th-century proponents of the concept are, for example, Doctors Charles Littlefield and his vital magnetism and George Starr White and his cosmo-electric energy. Mechanistic science in the 17th through 19th centuries embraced many of its essential qualities in the concept of the ether, while mystical human beings have embraced other essential qualities of it in the concept of god.

"Wilhelm Reich was the scientist who discovered orgone energy and developed the science of Orgonomy. He was born in 1897 and died in 1957. His scientific work spans the period from the 1920's through the 1950's. He spent most of his life scientifically researching the basic truth that underlies the character makeup of man and how it relates to his environment. ... Orgonomy is the scientific study of orgone (life energy) energy in living organisms, the Earth, and the atmosphere as well as outer space. Orgone energy is best described as a pre-atomic (mass-free) energy. Its natural flow is vital to a healthy individual as well as life on Earth."

THE PRANA PROGRAM
Enjoyable & Effective Evolution with Jasmuheen
e-book at http://www.selfempowermentacademy.com.au/htm/cia-education.asp#pranaprogram

Q: What is the difference between The Prana Program and the Solar nourishment program that you discuss in Chapter 8?

A: Solar nourishment is one way of obtaining micro food via our physical sun. It is ingested directly into the brain through the eyes and also through the pores of the skin. Hence as an external source of prana it is a small part of The Prana Program. However the feeding mechanisms we have been researching absorb and attract more prana from the inner planes, inter-dimensionally, and this way keeps us free from any external dependencies for nourishment as we draw prana through the atoms magnetizing cosmic particles to us via our resonance.

PRANA PROGRAM BENEFITS

Q: What are some of the personal benefits of increasing the pranic flow through the body?

Physical Benefits:- Body operates differently so we can gain the freedom to:
   a) Cease to create dis-ease on all levels;
   b) decrease our dependancy on the worlds food resources and no longer need to take physical nourishment from food if this is our inclination;
   c) decrease sleep dependancy and so provide us with more time;
   d) decrease our dependancy on world's water resources, even to the degree of eliminating our need for external fluid;
   e) stop the aging process as our body is fed by a purer source of nutrition.

Emotional Benefits:-
   a) Increases emotional sensitivity; feelings of Oneness, joy, inner and outer peace;
   b) increases feelings of passion and purpose and feeling fulfilled and fed on deep emotional levels;
   c) increases feelings of an internal, limitless, unconditional love which eliminates feelings of fear, loneliness and separation.

Mental Benefits:-
   a) Increases mental clarity;
   b) increases creativity;
   c) increases consciousness and awareness of the bigger picture in life,
   d) provides easier access to our inate wisdom, knowing and intuitive power.

Spiritual Benefits:-

a) Increasing the pranic flow can provide the experience of Oneness and interconnectedness of life;
b) increases our experience of enlightenment – being filled with light and joy;
c) increases our intuitive clairaudient, clairsentient and clairvoyant abilities;
d) increases our respect for all life;
e) easier to recognize the Divine plan and purpose to life and all roles within it;
f) easier to understand the true essence of the teaching's of all spiritual messengers Christ, Buddha, Mohammed etc.

Q: What other benefits did you personally experience when you learnt to be nourished purely by increasing your internal pranic flow?

A: One of the first benefits that I felt was incredible lightness of being, feeling vast, highly energized, expanded, multi-dimensional. These are the characteristics of the Divine spark within and, as we is allow this Divine limitless spark within – and without – to sustain us, we then take on its qualities. Having also existed now for over a decade on an average of less than 300 calories per day I have gained a greater appreciation of exactly what my body is capable of particularly as I have also experienced all of the benefits of the previous questions and so write from experience.

PRANA AND THE PHYSICAL BIO-SYSTEM

Q: Exactly what effects does The Prana Program have on health?

A: To me health means being physically, emotionally, mentally and spiritually healthy, and radiating frequencies that feed both ourselves and the world in a harmonious and beneficial manner. In 1900 the average western person lived to be 47 years old. Today it is approximately 76. Once people hit 40 they enter the zone of heart disease, cancer, strokes, diabetes, arthritis, osteoporosis and Alzheimer's disease. These seven illnesses will be responsible for the preventable deaths of more than 2 million North Americans in 2000. A well tuned bio-system with a strong pranic flow acts as a preventative medicine measure freeing us from dis-ease.

Q: How does a person maintain health on prana only nourishment if this becomes their choice?

A: It is all to do with flow. Everyone's bio-system produces prana naturally, how much it can produce, attract, hold and radiate through the system will determine how healthy they remain on a prana only nourishment program. For people whose systems are overloaded with toxicity maintaining health on a prana only food regime would not be possible.

Q: Why do we have a stomach and teeth if we are not meant to eat physical food?

A: Our current digestive system has evolved over time to mirror our beliefs and as these change so will our digestive system. The fact is that we can do anything we choose when we merge again into the stream of our DOW's power, for we are the masters of our own body, and as such every cell of our body is constantly listening to our thoughts, words and actions to which the molecules and atoms then adjust themselves in response. As we are the first generation of light eaters in the west we are also dependant upon the process of evolution for the inner system to change. However in time the future generations of light eater's internal circuitry will end up quite different so the short answer to this question is that it is just a matter of evolution, and time, and our body's ability to mirror our beliefs and practices. Those who continue to eat will keep their current digestive systems and those who choose Divine Nutrition will eventually have a digestive system that reflects this new way of being nourished.

It is said that when we first took form on this planet we had a different bio-system that was self-sustaining and needed neither food nor fluid; we have evolved over time to our current system and our future bio-system evolution depends on our lifestyle and choices. With re-education and experiential prana program awareness, over time our internal feeding structures will evolve differently, and eventually the new Prana Program feeding mechanisms will merge from the etheric to the physical and we will see biological changes to support our new way of feeding.

Q: How is prana transformed into gross matter to support and sustain the body's anatomy and physiology?

A: Prana is to God like sunshine is to the sun; both are natural by-products of something Radiant. It's everywhere already existing as Earth prana, air prana and cosmic prana and doesn't need transforming – it feeds everything anyway. We just forgot that it does so. Over our evolutionary process we have come to expect food to do the job instead.

Because the body already knows that prana is its natural source of food, it gets quite relieved when we – as masters of the body – know this also. It's kind of like sacking a dish wash person to replace them with an automatic dishwasher. Eating pranic light is just easier and quicker and cleaner. Also the body prefers it as it can then stop the complicated process of digestion and redirect its precious energy for other matters. All food has prana and when we eat, we absorb this into ourselves, but we can also learn how to by-pass the middle man and go straight to the Source.

Q: How does a prana only nourishment affect life expectancy? Is it a fountain of youth or does a person still age?

A: I cannot speak for all pranic nourishers, only of my personal journey, where in my reality physical immortality can go hand in hand with the pranic nourishment issue. Giri Bala of India, and Therese Neumann who bore the stigmata of Christ, were both pranic nourishers who aged gracefully and died. Being a pranic nourisher does not guarantee physical immortality unless one reprograms the pineal and pituitary glands to only produce life-sustaining hormones and also release limiting mortality patterns.

Also in order to be physically immortal one needs to let go of the belief system that one has to die, and release from the energy fields of the bodies all toxicity of thought, emotion and dietary substance. It is a path of purification, and being the most sublimely tuned instrument in the orchestra of the divine, and manifesting this into physical reality. Therefore accessing the fountain of youth depends on one's mind set and the release of our mortality patterns.

Q: Why are so many people focused a physical immortality?

A: Many people see themselves as the masters of their body and not slaves to it. It is their intention to fulfill their life purpose and then take the body up into light or drop it when they have completed their work rather than have it breakdown and then die from neglect or abuse.

Q: How does it affect physical beauty? Does increasing our pranic flow change our appearance?

A: A small number of people have the shamanic shape-shifting ability and can change the physical appearance at will. To me physical beauty is not the issue, vibrational beauty is and the most beautiful people I meet are those who are radiating the love and wisdom of the Divine force that breathes them. You can tell how strongly the pranic force is flowing in a body by the light in a person's eyes for our eyes are the windows to our soul.

Q: Why do people's sleep requirements decrease when they are anchored in The Prana Program?

A: As mentioned before, increasing the pranic flow changes the way our physical system operates as we need less energy for the digestion of food hence the body's energy levels change and it naturally requires less sleep. For the malnourished person the opposite is true.

THE PRANA PROGRAM
Enjoyable & Effective Evolution with Jasmuheen
e-book at http://www.selfempowermentacademy.com.au/htm/cia-education.asp#pranaprogram

***

Q: You often say that the ability to no longer need physical food is just one small benefit of maximizing the pranic flow through a body. Why is this when this benefit alone potentially has such a huge impact on our evolution, particularly regarding global resources?

A: Personally I feel that we need to maintain a correct perspective regarding the gifts that increasing the pranic flow can deliver. Over the last decade there has been too much sensationalism particularly by the media regarding the non-eating aspect that comes with The Prana Program. This focus has overshadowed the other benefits of The Prana Program that are more beneficial to our world today, most especially the emotional and mental benefits.

Q: Why do doctors and nutritionists say that people who do not take physical food will die and that living on prana is impossible? Are they wrong?

A: Everything doctors and nutritionists say is true for a person who maintains:-
   a) Beta level brain activity and
   b) physical, emotional, mental and spiritual toxicity.

As soon as we eliminate physical, emotional, mental and spiritual toxicity and anchor our brain wave pattern into the Alpha then Theta and Delta levels, our bio-system begins to function differently and in a way still unexplained by our doctors and nutritionists who tend to deal primarily with the physical systems needs rather than on holistic and more metaphysical levels.

Q: What is the difference between fasting and living on prana apart from the fact that both take no physical food?

A: With fasting we live off of body fat, as the system is flushed out and supported to detoxify itself, if continued for too long we see muscle shrinkage, rapid aging of the system as it begins to collapse from lack of nourishment and if prolonged further, eventual death. With prana we are simply feeding a body in a different way providing it with superior quality vitamins and minerals from an unseen and seemingly unexplainable nourishment source. Fasting is abstinence from food; pranic nourishment is eating in a different way from an alternate source.

Q: Many people do a lot of hard physical labor or exercise. Surely they need solid food to fulfill this function?

A: People sometimes think that in order to expend a lot of energy, as in physically demanding work that they need to have a good supply of food to provide the fuel of energy to expend. Firstly quality of fuel choice is important and the higher the quality, the less quantity is often required and the highest quality food source we have is prana. Secondly if the body is able to access and digest its food source with minimum energy expenditure, then it will have more energy to use for other things.

Our experiential research has found that people on The Prana Program get stronger, need less sleep, are more mentally alert and physically active which is the opposite of what most people expect so we are better at performing hard physical labor than we used to be.

Q: Many people who live on a prana only nourishment system find that their choice makes many people angry, why does this happen?
A: It challenges people's beliefs, beliefs that are set due to experience and education – when these are limited so are our beliefs. New education plus new experiences equals new beliefs in understanding and less anger from fear and ignorance. Remember western history has always seen the acquisition of food to be essential for survival and civilizations have formed around our food, water and our shelter needs. The hunting and gathering reality is firmly anchored in our collective psyche and so to now provide information from the eastern yogic traditions about being able to tap into an alternative source of nourishment – called prana – that is within us, can be a little challenging to people's fixed beliefs. Holistic education will alleviate this in time.

Q: Some people say that a lot of your research focuses too much on the physical body – is this so and is there a reason for this?
A: Unlike the Fakir's in India who would push their bodies to extremes, or other eastern philosophy traditions that tend to focus entirely on the spiritual journey and ignore the body, I believe that the physical body is a precious temple. Precious because it is home to our DOW whose love, radiation and gifts we can experience directly with our seven senses.

Also while we exist multi-dimensionally and for most of the time – except during sleep and deep meditation – our consciousness is anchored in the physical system. We are here right now for a purpose – whatever people deem this purpose to be – and maximizing the joy of the journey of this life helps with a well tuned bio-system.

THE PRANA PROGRAM AND THE DIVINE ONE WITHIN (THE DOW)

Q: Most of your research manuals focus on DOW power in some way. What is the DOW and what is its power?
A: Our Dow is the Divine One Within us – it is an energy field that incorporates our higher self and our I AM presence which is also called the Atman or the Monad. It is immortal, eternal in its

expression, limitless in its love and wisdom and is all seeing, all knowing and what some would call the God within.

Those who have sought to experience this 'inner God' have discovered that it is a force that can heal – as in Reiki and Pranic Healing; that it can guide us through our 6th and 7th senses of intuition and knowing; that it can pulse waves of nourishing love through us when we meditate on it and that it can nourish us on all levels, to the degree of even feeding us physically. These are some of it gifts and powers.

Many now believe that there is a force that is all knowing, all loving, existing everywhere within us and around us. This is the force that I call our DOW. It is incorruptible and the one force that we have in common, independent of our religions and beliefs, for it breathes us whether we acknowledge it or not. Experiencing its love is the key to eternal happiness and true fulfillment.

THE PRANA PROGRAM AND THE HEART

Q: How important is the heart chakra in The Prana Program?
A: The heart chakra is the doorway between worlds. When the sacral, crown and heart chakra are fully activated they expand to magnetize more cosmic particles into the bio-system.

The heart chakra is the major access point through which Divine Love, as pure prana, flows. It is also the anchor point for the Divine One Within – our DOW – or master computer controller of the bio-system – to express itself into this dimension.

Q: In your book The Law of Love you talk a lot about the heart chakra and heart qualities. Can you briefly discuss the more relevant points here?
A: We know that our DOW anchors itself in our heart chakra and then spreads Its rays out from the inner planes into our physical world, weaving Itself through our organs, light-body, meridians, bloodlines, skeleton and whole bio-system to support our system into a continuous stream of life. We know that the more powerfully It can radiate through us the healthier we are just as we know that when our DOW withdraws Its rays our physical system can no longer exist and therefore dies.

We also know that the more powerfully our DOW can harmoniously radiate Itself through our heart and our physical system and into our world, the more Grace we will experience and the more miracles. We also know that a harmonious heart has a huge influence in tuning us to the fields of freedom.

Heart

THE PRANA PROGRAM
Enjoyable & Effective Evolution with Jasmuheen
e-book at http://www.selfempowermentacademy.com.au/htm/cia-education.asp#pranaprogram

Q: The research in **The Law of Love** *combines some of the Taoist traditions; can you share more on these?*

A: According to the Taoists, the heart is an organ that holds the emotions of arrogance and compassion, hence for the rebalancing of a person or culture that is arrogant, the system needs to be inspired to be more compassionate. Being compassionate floods the heart with this emotion and changes its frequency field which, via the process of entrainment brings all the organs into a state of harmony.

In his book *Cosmic Inner Smile* Taoist Master Mantak Chia states: "Compassion is the highest expression of human emotion and virtuous energy. It is a level of development that takes hard work and serious meditation before it can blossom into one's life. It is not a single virtue, but the distillation and culmination of all virtues, expressed at any given moment as a blend of fairness, kindness, gentleness, honesty, respect, courage and love. It is the most beneficial energy to share with others. The power to express any or all of these virtues at the appropriate moment indicates that a person has internally unified him or herself into a state of compassion."

Q: And what about the entrainment effect that you found the Institute of HeartMath had researched?

A: In the book *The HeartMath Solution*, authors Doc Childe and Howard Martin explain how the electromagnetic fields radiating from the heart affect the fields around us, they also show us how to move into sensing life with the intuitive nature of our heart's brain rather than operating only from cranium's brain of limited linear thinking.

They say that "Heart intelligence is the intelligent flow of awareness and insight that we experience once the mind and the emotions are brought into balance and coherence through a self initiated process. This form of intelligence is experienced as direct intuitive knowing that manifests in thoughts and emotions that are beneficial for our selves and for others." (page 6 of HMS). HeartMath research shows that:

- ♥ "Because the heart is the strongest biological oscillator in the human system, the rest of the body's systems are pulled into entrainment with the hearts rhythms." (page 46 HMS)
- ♥ The quickest way to harmonize human heart rhythms is to focus on what the IHM call core heart feelings such as love and compassion.
- ♥ The heart has its own independent nervous system that is called "the brain in the heart".
- ♥ There are at least forty thousand neurons – nerve cells in the heart and these relay information back and forth to the brain in the cranium to allow for a two way communication

between our heart and brain, although the heart beats independently of its connection with the cranium brain.

- Research by Joel and Beatrice Lacey at the Fels Research Institute in the 1970's found **that when the cranium brain sent signals to the heart through the nervous system, our heart didn't automatically obey.** The hearts response depended on the nature of the task and the type of mental processing it required. However **the brain obeys all messages and instructions sent to it by the heart**, messages that could influence a person's behavior.

- The Fels Institute found that the heart beat is not just a mechanical throb but a system of intelligent language that influences our perception and reactions. Other researchers have found that the hearts rhythmic beating triggers neural impulses that influence the higher brain centers that govern emotional processing.

- Research at the IHM has also found that negative emotions disrupt the heart's rhythms so that they become jagged and disordered. They found that positive emotions produce smooth harmonious heart rhythms which in turn increase a person's mental clarity, intuition and ability to perceive the world more clearly as well as enhancing their communication with others.

- Being able to sustain balanced and harmonious heart rhythms allows a person to sustain a positive life perspective and intuitive flow and to access positive emotions at will.

- **The electromagnetic field of the heart is approximately 5000 times greater in strength than the electromagnetic field produced by the brain.** It not only permeates every cell of our body but is powerful enough to radiate out into the field around us a radiation that can be measured by magnetometers.

- The difference between heart and head intelligence is that the heart is open to intuitive solutions and the head is open to linear and logical solutions. When they work together we again have more choices in life and a clearer vision of how to fulfill our dreams. Coherence between the head and heart also allows us to operate more effectively through all fields of life – a fact that the IHM has tested repeatedly.

Q: And the IHM research has relevance to The Prana Program because?
A: While we can be the master of our mind and learn to work in a positive way with both our perceptions and our emotions, we cannot be the master of our heart, only its partner, yet accessing our heart's intelligence or its codes allows us to live life in full mastery.

According to research at the IHM "our feelings affect the information contained in the heart's electromagnetic signals" (page 59 HMS) and spectral analysis has revealed that when the heart's rhythms become more coherent and ordered then so does its electromagnetic field emanations, emanations that they have also found *can influence other peoples' brain wave patterns*. Spectral analysis can determine the mix of frequencies present in a field i.e. an electromagnetic fields ingredients.

Emotions such as appreciation and compassion create heart coherence just as anger and frustration create incoherence, consequently as we alter our perceptions in life, we alter our emotional flow which in turn alters our physical heart rhythms and allows us to alter our internal and external radiation levels and increase or decrease pranic flow.

Choosing to see the perfection of each situation, choosing to see the Divine spark in all, choosing to enjoy the fullness and simplicity of each moment, all of this alters our heart rhythm and our rhythm in our world and the type of rhythms that return to surround us and move through us. Research at the IHM has found that "when a system is coherent, virtually no energy is wasted, because its component parts are operating in sync." (page 63 HMS). http://www.heartmath.org/

PRANA AS EMOTIONAL, MENTAL AND SPIRITUAL FOOD

Q: How can prana feed the emotional body, and what benefits are there with this?
A: The human emotional body is constantly seeking nourishment and is naturally open, and attracted, to love. Our educational and cultural systems guide us to look at self love, family love, romantic love and even unconditional love and unfortunately these systems often negate the power and influence of Divine Love, which is the source of all love that we can know. One of the base essences of prana is Divine Love, or what some term the Madonna Frequency, and to experience Its increased flow within us feeds and fulfills us in unimaginable ways.

What many have forgotten and take for granted is the reason that we are being breathed. Something, some energy force, has control over our breathing mechanism and loves us enough to keep this pulsing so that we may experience life. When this energy withdraws Its love and focus from the bio-system it dies and no amount of oxygen will bring back life.

Deciding to experience the emotional gifts of the intelligence that exists behind the breath, that is breathing us, is a very nourishing and rewarding journey. What the ancient yogi's understood is that when we match our beat to the rhythm of the One breathing us those feelings of love increase. Merging with It consciously reveals a depth and breadth to our emotional spectrum that is unavailable to us if all we focus on is self love, family love or romantic love.

Ignoring something doesn't make it non-existent, it just tends to limit our experience of it. Focusing on Divine Love, which is the love our higher, more Divine nature has for us, is what delivers the emotional benefits of:-

- ☺ increased emotional sensitivity so that we can enjoy
- ☺ increased feelings of Oneness, joy plus inner and outer peace;
- ☺ increased feelings of passion and purpose and feeling fulfilled and fed on deep emotional levels;
- ☺ increased feelings of limitless love.

Q: How is prana utilized as mental food?

A: Firstly chi follows mind, so wherever we focus our mind we will find an influx of chi or prana following and flooding into the area that we are focused upon. Chi is like a puppy dog that is curious to see what its master is focused on and so follows its master everywhere.

So increasing the pranic flow:-

- ☺ activates the areas of the brain not used in basic survival issues;
- ☺ increases clarity;
- ☺ increases creativity;
- ☺ increases intuition and knowing as when directed it can further activate and feed the pituitary and pineal glands;
- ☺ brings in the 'like attracts like' paradigm, as our brain wave patterns change which changes how the U.F.I. responds to us;
- ☺ expands consciousness and activates super conscious or higher mind.
- ☺ Also the violet light aspect of prana responds to programming as Chi flows where mind goes.

Q: How can we use prana as spiritual food and what are the benefits – personally and globally – of doing so?

A: Some benefits of this are:-

- ☺ Increases unification by increasing feelings of Oneness and personal fulfillment;
- ☺ provides a common bond of experience of our Divine essence that takes us beyond religious ideologies and doctrine thus providing unity and tolerance;
- ☺ increases creative flow and stimulates higher brain centers which expands consciousness and knowing of higher realities and our place within it thus providing more harmonious global and universal paradigms;

- ☺ promotes internal and external intergration, balance and harmony and thus increases our feelings of inner and outer peace;
- ☺ changes the frequencies we radiate so we feed the world rather than drain it.

Q: What is the simplest science to understanding how The Prana Program's benefits can be manifested?

A: Prana Program benefits are experienced:-
- ☺ when we understand that we are all just systems of energy that can be tuned or untuned;
- ☺ when we consciously change our brain wave patterns via how we spend our time i.e. what we focus upon and our lifestyle;
- ☺ when we understand and apply the Universal Law of Resonance;
- ☺ when we apply effective mind power by mastering our thinking patterns, eliminating limited beliefs and
- ☺ when we consciously work in harmony with Universal Mind and its infinite field of love and wisdom.

Q: What is the simplest procedure a person needs to adopt for gaining The Prana Program benefits?

- ☺ Firstly, become educated in The Prana Program and its power;
- ☺ next learn breathing patterns and understand all you can about breath power;
- ☺ also understand mind power and how to use it to attract and absorb cosmic particles.
- ☺ In addition, apply the internal feeding mechanisms and program outlined in the last section of this book;
- ☺ and bring yourself into a state of physical, emotional, mental and spiritual fitness via your lifestyle, perceptions and belief choices.
- ☺ Finally, understand about and then adjust your personal calibration.

Q: What are some other benefits of being sustained by prana that you have personally experienced?

A: The process of digestion utilizes energy, when this is no longer required this energy can be redirected for other purposes. So for me, it seemed to enhance my creativity and expand my inter-dimensional telepathic abilities. Due to my daily lifestyle choice, and what it entails, it is impossible to separate what is responsible for the magic I now experience daily in my existence as meditation, strong inner guidance, focusing on my own harmonious evolution, and service, while existing on prana all are interwoven. The Prana Program has led me to understand more about the power of mind over matter, mortality patterns, limitless being and self mastery, ascension, the path of enlightenment, being in service to a greater more loving paradigm and so much more.

Q: Are there any other benefits that people have reported?

A: Yes one other benefit of The Prana Program, and increasing the prana flow through our systems, is that it gives us the food we need to remember and awaken to our true nature. I tend to liken the experience of awakening to our DOW (however we may choose to remember and awaken to It) as finally getting to play with the 'big kid' (for our Divine nature is a more civilized being of great light and love) who happens to know all the tricks and have all the fun! It is all knowing, all powerful, all loving and all wise and exists through all time, space and dimensions.

Also The Prana Program often stimulates us to master the physical, emotional and mental bodies and to integrate these bodies into one complete, Divine whole that works in unison to express our maximum potential harmoniously. Although the benefits of inceasing the pranic flow manifests most obviously in the physical body, one must really also continue with intense work on both the emotional and mental bodies while being guided by our inner spiritual being throughout the whole conversion process.

Regardless of how we choose to achieve it, many now believe that all beings upon this plane at this time must eventually complete their learning cycle and master themselves and bring their being back into perfect alignment with their DOW. It is my reality that this process of awakening and self mastery is no longer a matter of choice, for the planet is on a destined course for a more enjoyable and effective evolution.

THE PRANA PROGRAM AND THE BRAIN

Q: Can you share a little more about general brain wave research?

A: Information on http://www.mhhe.com/biosci/ap/vdgconcepts/student/olc/n-reading13.html says that: "Brain waves are recordings of fluctuating electrical changes in the brain. To obtain such a recording, electrodes are positioned on the surface of a surgically exposed brain (an electrocardiogram, ECG) or on the outer surface of the head (an electroencephalogram, EEG). These electrodes detect electrical changes in the extracellular fluid of the brain in response to changes in potential among large groups of neurons. The resulting signals from the electrodes are amplified and recorded. Brain waves originate from the cerebral cortex, but also reflect activities in other parts of the brain that influence the cortex, such as the reticular formation. Because the intensity of electrical changes is directly related to the degree of neuronal activity, brain waves vary markedly in amplitude and frequency between sleep and wakefulness." Study of brain wave patterns have led to the discovery of the Beta, Alpha, Theta and Delta fields.

Q: Why is refining brain wave activity so important in The Prana Program?
A: Our experience has been that when the brain wave patterns move into Alpha, then Theta, then Delta patterns, many other realities begin to emerge (for example, the ability to be healthily nourished by Divine Love – chi or prana – comes from being anchored in the Theta/Delta worlds). The more we increase the pranic flow through a bio-system, the better it functions and brain wave activity automatically changes via the lifestyle we need to do this. Meditation brings us through the Alpha-Theta-Delta levels where cosmic particles are more easily magnetized to us.

Q: Can you describe some of the attributes of the different brain wave patterns?
A: With brain wave patterns resonating at 14-30 cycles per second, the Beta field is the field of poverty, violence, social injustice, emotional highs and emotional lows, and is often a field of man-made, self-inflicted chaos and victim consciousness. It is the beat of 'busy'ness.

Resonating at 8-13 cycles per second, the Alpha field begins to reveal the Zen of life, allowing us down time, to chill out and effectively see and reset the direction of our life and to recognize and assess the imbalances and re-address them, hopefully for the good of all. Time in the Alpha zone via meditation improves our health and happiness levels and is step one in the direct and conscious feeding of our being in a new way.

With brain wave patterns resonating at 4-7 cycles per second, the Theta field brings co-incidences that no longer seem to be random and time spent here attracts events filled with symbolism and deep, meaningful possibilities for it is a field of infinitely creative potential, a field of Grace, true nourishment and love. This is the field through which all Holiness and true messengers come. This is the zone from which all the Holy books were born after being downloaded telepathically from the universal field of Infinite love and wisdom whose main rhythm is Theta.

Resonating at ½ - 3 cycles per second, the Delta fields bring it all, for from its field springs paradise and the 'garden of Eden' of the Bible's God. The Delta zone is also the home of the Elohim and the Archangels and pure love. It is the home from where our supernatural abilities flow and it is where our DOW is anchored to radiate out through our form. It is often accessed in deep meditation and is experienced more powerfully within a toxin free system. This is the field the yogi's dwell in when they leave their bodies to experience inter-dimensional cosmic traveling.

THE PRANA PROGRAM
Enjoyable & Effective Evolution with Jasmuheen
e-book at http://www.selfempowermentacademy.com.au/htm/cia-education.asp#pranaprogram

Q: What role does the pituitary gland play in The Prana Program?

A: As one of the master glands of the body, the eastern mystics found that the pituitary gland produces a food called amrita which they claim is the fountain of youth. When the pituitary gland is stimulated via certain tongue positions and via flooding with violet light and programming with specific intention, it increases its production of amrita which feeds the brain what it needs to simulate the neuro-theology buttons and hence influence brain wave patterns.

Also, according to Ancient Wisdoms, when the pituitary and pineal glands are activated, our brain wave patterns lock themselves more permanently into Alpha spectrum and when they move into Theta and Delta zones we begin to use the rest of our previously under utilized brains.

Q: What role does the pineal gland play in The Prana Program?

A: The pineal gland when stimulated, using similar tools to the above plus other Taoist methods, will increase its production of a substance called pinoline which also feeds the brain and increases the production of the neurohormones DMT and 5-MeO-DMT. When a bio-system is free from physical, emotional and mental toxicity and these hormones are increasing, the system begins to operate in a different way revealing our natural more alchemical type abilities.

Q: Why do we use only 10-20% of our brain capacity?

A: Firstly it only takes a small percentage of our brain to address and fulfill our survival needs. The balance of our brain lies dormant as focusing only on survival restricts our internal pranic flow which in turn restricts what sections of our brain are activated to fulfill their higher potential. What we don't use in the brain simply lies dormant until we do.

Q: How do we use prana to activate the areas of the brain that we don't use for physical survival?

A: There are various ways to do this. For example, by flooding our brain with violet light we can feed brain function and stimulate it to respond in a different way but generally these sections of the brain are automatically activated as we recalibrate ourselves via various lifestyle tools and holding certain mindsets.

Q: What about the science of neurotheology?

A: Neurotheology has found that various areas of the brain, when activated by certain procedures, download feelings of bliss, ecstasy, religious fervor and revelation; e.g. the temporal lobe has a joy button, the parietal lobe connects us with feelings of oneness and unity, the occipital lobe allows us to process sacred images. Bliss brain waves can be experienced by the use of mantras, prayer, chanting, meditation, visualization and breathing techniques.

Q: Anything else on the brain that is relevant to The Prana Program?
A: Yes according to research done by the Maharishi and the TM movement, 7000 people holding a constant 8hz brain wave pattern can transform our world into harmony. Increasing the pranic flow automatically increases personal and global harmony as it puts the brain into the 8hz pattern.

PRANA AND DARKROOM TECHNOLOGY

Q: Over the last few years you have begun the practice of darkroom therapy, why is that?
A: According to Mantak Chia, "The darkness actualizes successively higher states of divine consciousness, correlating with the synthesis and accumulation of psychedelic chemicals in the brain. Melatonin, a regulatory hormone, quiets the body and mind in preparation for the finer and subtler realities of higher consciousness (Days 1 to 3). Pinoline, affecting the neuro-transmitters of the brain, permits visions and dream-states to emerge in our conscious awareness (Days 3 to 5). Eventually, the brain synthesizes the "spirit molecules" 5-methoxy-dimethyltryptamine (5-MeO-DMT) and dimethyltryptamine (DMT), facilitating the transcendental experiences of universal love and compassion (Days 6 to 12)." So during a darkroom retreat we can experience the benefits of different brain functions.

Q: You have also been combining this darkroom practice with The Prana Program, how does this work?
A: A darkroom retreat-type situation is a wonderful way to create and/or expand specific internal feeding mechanisms and to check their success as we unhook from all external light and physical food absorption.

Q: What are some at the other benefits of darkroom retreats and The Prana Program that you share there?
A: Apart from what we have already explained, the darkroom experience has numerous benefits for the participant. Firstly it recreates an experience of being in the Divine Mother's womb from where all light flows, next it eliminates feelings of separation as all you see and/or feel is that you are an

individual point of consciousness. While I have spoken at length of my first darkroom experience in the free e-book "Darkroom Diary Downloads" at:

http://www.selfempowermentacademy.com.au/htm/files/e-Books-free/Darkroom-Downloads.pdf, deprivation of physical sight, like the deprivation of physical food, allows our other bio-system abilities to be revealed especially when we utilize the darkroom time of silence and solitude to explore even deeper the inner planes of consciousness.

PRANA AND THE CELLS

Before we look at things like cellular pulsing and its relevance to The Prana Program, we need to also understand a little more regarding cellular function. The below data is humorous and offered in layman's terms and comes from Bill Bryson's book: *A Short History of Nearly Everything*.

"It starts with a single cell. The first cell splits to become two and the two become four and so on … And every one of those cells knows exactly what to do to preserve and nurture you from the moment of conception to your last breath."

"You have no secrets from your cells. They know far more about you than you do. Each one carries a copy of the complete genetic code – the instruction manual for your body – so it knows how to do not only its own job but every other job in the body too."

"Your cells are a country of ten thousand trillion citizens, each devoted in some intensively specific way to your overall well-being. There isn't a thing they don't do for you. They let you feel pleasure and form thoughts."

"Most living cells seldom last more than a month or so, but there are some notable exceptions. Liver cells can survive for years, though the components within them may be renewed every few days. Brain cells last as long as you do. You are issued with a hundred billion or so at birth and that is all you are ever going to get. It has been estimated that you lose five hundred of them an hour, so if you have any serious thinking to do there really isn't a moment to waste. The good news is that the individual components of your brain cells are constantly renewed so that, as with the liver cells, no part of them is actually likely to be more than about a month old."

"When cells are no longer needed, they die with what can only be called great dignity. They take down all the struts and buttresses that hold them together and quietly devour their component parts. The process is known as apoptosis or programmed cell death. Every day billions of your cells die for your benefit and billions of others clean up the mess. Cells can also die violently – for instance, when infected – but mostly they die because they are told to. Indeed, if not told to live – if not given some kind of active instruction from another cell – cells automatically kill themselves. Cells need a lot of reassurance."

"The wonder of cells is not that things occasionally go wrong, but that they manage everything so smoothly for decades at a stretch. They do so by constantly sending and monitoring streams of messages – a cacophony of messages – from all around the body: instructions, queries, corrections, requests for assistance, updates, and notices to divide or expire. Most of these signals arrive by means of couriers called hormones, chemical entities such as insulin, adrenaline, estrogen and testosterone that convey information from remote outposts like the thyroid and endocrine glands. Still other messages arrive by telegraph from the brain or from regional centers in a process called paracrine signalling. Finally, cells communicate directly with their neighbours to make sure their actions are coordinated."

Q: Apart from being interesting information, what relevance is the above data to The Prana Program?

A: Basically that cells are programmed by hormones, chemicals and others cells and can also be reprogrammed consciously by our mind. They can be cleansed, they can be detoxified if toxic and they can learn to operate in a different way via new specific programming. I also provide the above data as the fact is that there is still so much that is not understood about cellular function.

Advocates of The Prana Program say that prana can deliver all nutrients, all vitamins, proteins and minerals to keep a system healthy and while some may find this difficult to believe, it isn't when we understand the nature of prana and its violet light essence. Nor is it incomprehensible when we realize as Bill Bryson's research shares: "You have at least 20,000 different types of protein labouring away inside you and so far we understand what no more than 2 per cent of them do. (Others put the figure at more like 50 per cent; it depends, apparently, on what you mean by 'understand')." My point exactly.

Q: Can you discuss cellular pulsing and its impact on The Prana Program?

A: As discussed in my book *In Resonance*, we know that our cells store memories and emotions and act as our personal internal filing cabinet. We also know that each cell consists of atoms which consist of 99.99% space. We know also that this space is really pure Divine consciousness that is undetectable to the normal scientific measuring scopes, as DOW Power resonates at a frequency too refined to be detected by normal methods. For the purpose of this discussion I would like to call the beat of this Divine consciousness that fills each atom, our internal classical music station.

What I have also come to understand is that the more that our cells are filled with the emotional and mental toxicity of life, the weaker the Divine or classical music pulse in each cell is and yet how well we can be nourished purely by prana is totally dependant on the strength of the Divine pulse in each cell. Again for the purpose of this discussion I would like to refer to this cellular toxicity, that comes from our past emotional experiences and negative mental perceptions in life, as our internal heavy metal music station.

Q: Can you elaborate on this with an example?

A: Imagine two radios standing side by side, both switched on with one tuned to the classical music channel – our Divine pulse; the other tuned to a heavy metal music channel – our collective memory patterns. Assuming a maximum volume of 10, then if the classical music volume is playing at a 1 or a 2 and the heavy metal station is at a volume of 9 then we will definitely end up with the usual range of human limitations, diseases, decay and eventual death. However if these numbers are reversed and the Divine pulse of classical music is at a 7, 8, or 9 volume level and the toxic heavy metal channel is at a 1, 2, 3 volume level then the game and our experience in life becomes very different. A 9 to 1 ratio where the classical beat dominates, allows for pranic nutrition to occur much more easily, so our job is to empty the cells of toxic matter or transmute this 'heavy metal' matter into a purer frequency.

I heard someone say recently that research now shares that each cell has 6 gigabyte storage capacity. If this is true then our cells have huge storage capacity for many frequencies.

Q: How can we do this emptying or transmutation?

A: We can do this via a few methods. One is flooding the cells with violet light; the other is emptying the cells of unnecessary dross by freeing ourselves from both karmic debts and energy influences that no longer support us.

We can do this using a meditation with a focus on forgiveness.

An aware metaphysician knows that on one level everything is perfect, that there are no rights, no wrongs, and that all occurs to teach us and help us to develop and grow. However we didn't always have this type of awareness and so we hold in our cells lifetimes of hurts, angers, judgements and energies that hold a negative charge which takes up unnecessary space in our cells and keeps the heavy metal music station at a higher than healthy volume thus drowning out the more nurturing classical beat. Hence when we apply Forgiveness Meditation (Technique no. 23) in *The Food of Gods* book, and then flood the cells with the violet light, we reset the volumes to a more supportive pattern so that the cells can be nourished instead of depleted.

Q: You mentioned in your first book that there are changes happening in the DNA of many people, will this make living on a prana only nourishment routine easier?

A: There are many changes happening to many people. Metaphysically, we have within us the lightbody, and this contains encodements of information like files. When we ask the right questions this data is released. A lot of people have gone way beyond the point of asking questions like "why they are here, what's the meaning of life", etcetera, and have found very satisfying answers; they have reached an advanced stage of 'downloading' their encodements and are now very active in service here. The planet is changing drastically to reflect this.

If enough people believe something is true, it can be, as first in will, then in imagination, then in reality. We can all expand our consciousness and move into another energy band where we are all in harmony, as outer chaos is just a symbol of inner chaos. Part of The Prana Program agenda is about stimulating people's interest in creating another movie called "Thriving on planet Earth"; not just surviving and we can only do this when all basic human rights are taken care of. Changes in human DNA are reflecting the change in planetary consciousness. A recent survey found that 70% of US citizens admitted to having enjoyed a spiritual experience.

PRANA AND FIELD SCIENCE

Q: What is the science of the fields?

A: The science of the fields is the study of light ray and sound wave influences as they move through the dimensions of creation. It is also the study of universal laws, intentionally directed mind power and how observing and consciously programming a field can influence its formation. Hence it can cover research into personal, community, global, universal and even dimensional energy field emmanations and how these impact on each other and interrelate. It can also often cover our ability to either drain or feed an energy field by our presence. (We cover this in detail in the Biofields and Bliss trilogy)

Q: You often refer to prana also as Chi or Cosmic Particles and also as the Divine Love aspect of the Violet Light. Can you explain the differences if there are any?

A: The flow of prana can be felt as a vibration of love that is intuitively experienced to be divine in its limitless nature, as when it flows through the body every cell dances to its rhythm and feels complete and whole somehow. When one meditates on this river of love light, and looks at it through the third eye with our inner visionary capabilities, we can see its violet light hue.

Cosmic particles carry a perfect blend of seven elements that we know of – Earth, water, fire, air, astral light, akasha and cosmic fire and these create the perfect mix and flow of nourishment for the human system when it can attract enough of these particles for continued sustenance. My hypothesis is that it is the flow and blend of these elements that sustains health enough to be food free and that the element mix needs the perfect amount of astral light, akasha and cosmic fire.

The more a human system can vibrate to the resonance of Divine Love, the more prana or cosmic particles it attracts although the element mix we can attract will alter according to which dimension we anchor or expand ourselves into.

Q: What do you mean by 'dimension we anchor or expand ourselves into'?

A: Although as eternal beings of limitless love and infinite intelligence we exist through all dimensions simultaneously as part of a cosmic web of life, most people limit their conscious awareness to the 3rd dimensional plane of physical life on Earth. The more we expand and refine our consciousness to move through the higher dimensions, the more cosmic fire, akasha and astral light that we attract and radiate through our systems and the freer from human limitations we become. We cover more on the dimensions in my book *In Resonance*.

Q: You say that prana is the purest form of nourishment there is, why?

A: Due to its violet light essence, prana as cosmic particles provides the building blocks to create and then sustain all life. It holds within its essence all the forces of creation and contains all the elements required to create life – from molecular levels to vitamin and mineral levels. Hence it is pure and unlike a lot of modern day physical food it is free from food coloring, insecticides, pesticides and genetic modification. Therefore a prana only nourishment regime frees us of many modern day dietry concerns.

Q: What is the Violet Light and why is it so powerful?

A: Violet light is composed of three frequencies. The pink light that flows as waves of Divine Love as the original food that birthed and sustains all creation; golden white light as Divine Intelligence that carries all the mathematical codes and formulas required for creation to express itself through the dimensions and to operate the universal field; plus the blue aspect of Divine Power that provides the strength and impetus to create with love and wisdom and bring creative thought into tangible manifestation.

Using creative visualization, directed will and pure intention, violet light can be used in The Prana Program to flood a bio-system with cosmic particles for nutrition and also hydration, and if specifically programmed it can free the system from all human limitations such as the need to age, die or take external nourishment.

Q: How is the Violet Light utilized?
A: Used by master alchemists throughout time, violet light can be directed by thought, will and intention and telepathically programmed to provide specific outcomes as just mentioned. It can also be used as a basis for supportive or transmutative grid structures in the field of dimensional biofield science to prevent burn out of our electrical circuitry as we increase the pranic flow.

Q: What do you mean by 'burn out'?
A: It is not unusual for some people when they activate the kundalini energy that it can overwhelm the bio-system – due to its potency – and create problems with the circuitry of the body. Too much too soon can be damaging hence violet light grids can regulate the pranic (kundalini) flow.

Q: How else can the Violet Light be used?
A: As the visual aspect of the 7th ray of spiritual freedom, the violet light is currently being used for transformation – to alchemically merge the physical world with a non-physical etheric world of dreams where there is a higher, more harmonious paradigm of human expression. This is a world idealists and alchemists have willed into creation that is free of injustice or health and hunger issues and where prana power is understood and utilized for its obvious personal and global benefits.

Q: In the Biofields Series you talk a lot about Biofield Grids, Four Body Fitness and how these affect the pranic flow. Can you elaborate on this briefly here?
A: Biofield Grids form the basis of all fields and consist of light rays and sound waves which carry beneficial Coded information. Biofields and grids can only be seen by using the Language of Light which is the language of the Dimensional Biofield. The Language of Light is available to all who activate their 6th and 7th senses which we do by our daily lifestyle focus. Biofield Grids surround, and are woven through all life forms and the human bio-system has a supporting foundation of an inner Grid called the Lightbody that supports the meridian's and acupuncture points.

Q: Can you share more regarding the Lightbody and how it works with the pranic flow?
A: The Lightbody, as a matrix type web of energy, is the antenna for receiving signals from the fields and these signals come both inter-dimensionally and from a myriad of sources. Each Lightbody acts

as a radio and television station, constantly beaming out into the Social and Global Biofields, affecting each one by leaving an imprint of our resonance and also attracting back to us, via a system of biofeedback looping, exactly what we need. It is also encoded with all the blueprints and data we need for successful and effective co-creation.

In Dimensional Biofield Science, the energy received by the Lightbody flows through our sun and is stepped down in frequency to feed our body's meridians and chakra system. The level of energy that flows through these then determines our fitness levels, and the less blockages or restrictions to the flow, the healthier and happier we are. The voltage we can receive into our bio-system is determined by its capacity to receive.

Q: Can you share a little more of your research into field science?
A: As a higher light scientist, below is some of my understanding of the fields.

Firstly, in Biofield Science each field constantly influences the other, and how much influence each has depends upon the frequency of each individual. All fields are part of the Dimensional Biofield Grid and each grid contains a multitude of frequency patterns. Grid points are where light rays and sound waves cross. This is where consciousness tends to be drawn and coagulate and create what I call a "Grid Station". Successful Biofield Grid tuning needs to be practiced with discernment and requires us to know enough of all Grid Stations to choose our sources carefully and provide ways for us to magnetize more prana. Using Dimensional Biofield Science techniques, all Biofields can draw new frequencies through their own foundation Grids, and influence the frequency in each field and also feed fields.

Each Lightbody Biofield Grid has been pre-encoded in its DOS – the Divine Order System that supports all life in the Grid. Decoding this information brings true fulfillment in life as the Grid tuner eventually becomes better informed in the art of Dimensional Biofield Science.

Biofield Grids operate via energy transmissions that are governed by Universal Law.

Dimensional Biofield Grids and their subsequent transmission signals can be harmonized, or overhauled and completely retuned, by our application of RECIPE 2000> as discussed in the Biofields Series or by the data offered at:

http://www.selfempowermentacademy.com.au/htm/library.asp#recipe2000.

Q: How does field flow mastery effect evolution?
A: Our mastery of energy fields makes our creation more conscious and intentionally directed and able to determine more specific and desired outcomes. It allows us to move from exisiting in fields of random chaos, filled with or driven by victim consciousness, to acting as if we are intelligent creative

beings and experiencing the benefits that self knowledge and self mastery brings. We do this by a system that I call "field irradiation" or "flooding", which means allowing the intensity of our personal calibration to overwhelm and retune the surrounding fields.

Q: How does Quantum Physics relate to prana?
A: On a simplistic level, Quantum says that every atom is a door to a universe when we look at subatomic levels. It is through these inner atom doors that prana flows to feed us particularly when accessed via the type of internal violet light feeding mechanisms that we will discuss later.

Q: Can you define quantum in its more usual sense?
A: According to science and http://www.wordiq.com/definition/Quantum Physics, "Quantum mechanics is a fundamental physical theory which extends and corrects classical Newtonian mechanics, especially at the atomic and subatomic levels. It takes its name from the term quantum (Latin for "how much") used in physics to describe the smallest discrete increments into which something is subdivided. The terms quantum physics and quantum theory are often used as synonyms of quantum mechanics."

"Quantum mechanics describes with great accuracy and precision many phenomena where classical mechanics drastically fails to agree with experiments, including the behavior of systems of very small objects typically the size of atoms or smaller, but also some macroscopic phenomena, like superconductivity and superfluidity."

"It is the underlying framework of many fields of physics and chemistry, including condensed matter physics, quantum chemistry, and particle physics. The foundations of quantum mechanics were established during the first half of the 20th century by Max Planck, Albert Einstein, Niels Bohr, Werner Heisenberg, and others. Some fundamental aspects of the theory are still actively studied."

Q: You talk a lot in your research about resonance and the importance of being a tuned instrument so that we can magnetize enough pranic energy to nourish us on all levels. What exactly is resonance?
A: "In physics, resonance is an increase in the oscillatory energy absorbed by a system when the frequency of the oscillations matches the system's natural frequency of vibration (its resonant frequency). A resonant object, whether mechanical, acoustic, or electromagnetic, will probably have more than one resonant frequency (especially harmonics of the strongest resonance). It will be easy to vibrate at those frequencies, and more difficult to vibrate at other frequencies. It will "pick out" its resonant frequency from a complex excitation, such as an impulse or a wideband noise excitation.

In effect, it is filtering out all frequencies other than its resonance."
http://www.wordiq.com/definition/Resonance

The above also applies to the harmonics of a human bio-system which can be tuned and in perfect resonance with the universal field and hence attract maximum pranic flow or untuned and hence attract chaotic signatures that create and stimulate disease and disharmony.

Q: Do humans have a perfect resonance and if so how do we tune to it?

A: The perfect resonance of a human system is that of its original Divine DNA codes which is pure prana expressed as a Divine Love field filled with limitless potential. Realignment back to these natural signatures comes via our desire to know all aspects of our nature, via our conscious intention, and via our lifestyle and how we choose to spend our time.

Q: Where does the reality of reincarnation fit into The Prana Program or your personal model of it?

A: Personally I believe in the science of the indestructibility of energy, that energy cannot be created or destroyed but simply changes form. I also believe that humans are a system of energy that can be tuned to various realities and realms of experience. To me the heart that drives the human energy system is the immortal DOW – the Divine One Within – whose gifts and abilities are limitless. When we consciously tune more to its channel and less to the external world we become more effective and enjoy the evolutionary process in a deeper more profound and fulfilling way.

Q: What is the morphogenetic field?

A: This is the field that is the sum total of all life's vibratory signatures, i.e. every living things energy field all mixed into one soup of specific frequencies, with the dominant combination driving the field or holding it in set paradigms. As a field surrounding the planet, its imprint in the universal and inter-dimensional fields changes as human consciousness changes.

Q: Can prana be measured scientifically?

Answer with Eltrayan: In recent years substantial scientific testing has been done to establish the presence and nature of pranic emissions. However, the methodology of modern science stresses that the observer and the observed are separate and this is an essential feature of scientific observation. But traditional prana theory stresses that according to the most fundamental reasoning, the observed and the observer are in fact one, both consisting of prana, and are inseparable. Therefore, the observer alters what is observed by observing it, which is what in fact occurs at the level of quantum physics. This makes the accurate measurement of prana by traditional scientific methods difficult.

Q: What sort of other properties does the prana flow exhibit?

Answer with Eltrayan: Numerous scientific tests conducted by Chinese scientists have established the most remarkable properties of prana, e.g. prana has been proved to be able to penetrate walls and tens of metres of dense material. Consequently neutrons, neutrinos, gamma rays and x-rays were considered, because they had these properties. However, on testing it was found that prana was not exclusively any of these emissions.

The nature of the external prana has been studied in China for many years, involving almost all fields of modern physics such as infra-red radiation, ultra-violet radiation, electro-magnetic waves, micro waves, magnetic fields, neutrons, electron physics and so on. However, those who have participated in the experiments suggest that the properties of external prana are still far beyond what may have been studied. It is obvious that there are physical properties of external prana yet to be discovered due to the limitations of our current understanding of science and technology.

It was demonstrated that experiments using prana emissions can be conducted at a distance of 2,000km from the emitter of the prana to the experiment. This is difficult for science to comprehend. However, prana does not seem to obey the normal scientific rules pertaining to proportionality. It can probably be best compared with a laser beam which can travel long distances and not lose much intensity in its travels. The point seems to be that there is no evidence that external prana is a gravitational or electro-magnetic force, and therefore does not necessarily obey the scientific law of proportionality.

Note: All experiments regarding external pranic treatment have to be made with the external prana emitted by pranic masters, that is healers or teachers in the field. Prana emission consumes the prana master's vital energy, and is subject to their physical and mental conditions. As a result only similar, but not identical results can be obtained from different pranic emissions. Further, external pranic experiments often produce results that seem difficult to explain using modern scientific knowledge and demonstrate unusual phenomenon that are often beyond common sense.

Q: What other research has been done on prana emissions by the Chinese?

Answer with Eltrayan: Another scientific oddity is the paradox of being able to move solid objects through barriers. A simplistic explanation is that an object with one dimensional freedom can only move back and forth on a straight line. If there is an obstacle on the line, the object cannot pass it.

The object with two dimensional freedom however, can easily pass around it. For an object being only able to move in a two dimensional plane it will be stopped when it is surrounded by a circling obstacle. But an object with three dimensional freedom can easily get over this circling obstacle from above and move on.

It is natural to deduce that an object with four dimensional freedom will not be hindered by an obstacle in a three dimensional space. Therefore, pills sealed in a bottle, where the pills have four dimensional freedom, would not be impeded by the three dimensional bottle. The three dimensional pills enter into a fourth dimensional space the instant they receive external prana emitted by a prana master who has extraordinary functions.

A Chinese scientist from the Institute of Space Medical Engineering captured the whole process of pills escaping from a bottle using a high speed camera. He found one frame of film among several thousand frames showing half of a pill coming out of the side of the bottle and the following three frames showing the whole pill gradually dropping down. The observers suggested that the instant a pill receives the external prana emitted by the prana master, it enters into a state of virtual mass thereby passing through the bottle without resistance and afterwards turns back into its original real state – a pill. They of course have no explanation as to why the pill goes into a fourth dimensional space or virtual mass space, after receiving the external prana.

Q: What have scientific experiments concluded regarding pranic flow and emissions?
Answer with Eltrayan: The conclusion of many scientific experiments is that before external prana reaches the sample being tested it does not have a definite form or state such as infra-red radiation, gamma rays or neutrons, instead it only has the general characteristics of external prana, such as penetrating, targeting and bi-directionality. Only at the moment it reaches and touches the sample being tested does the external prana acquire the definite state corresponding to the conditions required to change this sample in a predetermined way. For example, external prana may act like ultra violet light, infra-red radiation or neutrons to affect the object. Scientists call this characteristic 'target-adaptability' of external prana.

Q: There are various models or processes for accessing the "living purely by prana state", can you share about these?
A: Yes below are the ones that I have personally experienced and also a few others that I am aware of.

1. The paths of Giri Bala and Therese Neuman as discussed in *An Autobiography of a Yogi*. For Giri her method was Kriya-Yoga and for Therese great faith, trust and love for, and in, the Divine.
2. The ancient yogi path as spoken of in Vedic literature – using again Kriya-Yoga and Pranayama processes of breath and light work.
3. Morris Krok using various lifestyle refinement methods as detailed in *Diet, Health, & Living On Air*.
4. Wiley Brooks in the early 1970's – I am unsure as to his exact model.
5. The 21 day process – as outlined in the book *Living on Light* – a spiritual initiation to increase the pranic flow, a small by-product of which can be the freedom from the need for physical food. **This model can be dangerous for the unprepared.**
6. Prahlad Jani's model of being fed and hydrated through a hole in his soft palette. As researched by Dr Sudhir Shah in Ahmedabad in India.
7. The model offered in the book *The Food of Gods* which combines lifestyle tools and Taoist and Vedic methods.
8. Hira Ratan Manek's Solar Nourishment method which we discuss in more detail later. As researched by Dr Sudhir Shah in Ahmedabad in India.
9. Zinaida Baranova's method of supreme trust, faith and love.
10. The model offered in *The Law of Love* that shares of a fluid and food free existence using ancient Taoist tools and futuristic science.
11. According to an ABC news story, there is also the case of the 15 year old Buddhist boy in Nepal called Ram Bahadur Banjan who has sat under a tree, in the jungle of Bara, since May 17th 2005 and as at the time of the story in November he had not eaten or drunk anything, nor spoken, for six months.

* Note: points 5, 7 & 10 are covered in Jasmuheen's manuals of the same names.

THE PRANA PROGRAM AND INTER-DIMENSIONAL LIFE

Q: What is inter-dimensional life?

A: It is the experience of our natural multi-dimensional nature that comes via a journey of expansion of our consciousness. By changing our brain wave patterns we can experience the different realities of more subtle and refined dimensions that exist within us and around us.

THE PRANA PROGRAM
Enjoyable & Effective Evolution with Jasmuheen
e-book at http://www.selfempowermentacademy.com.au/htm/cia-education.asp#pranaprogram

Q: Some people have criticized your first books on this due to your constant referencing to Holy Ones and Beings of Light. What relevance – if any – do they have to The Prana Program?

A: Nothing and also everything. Firstly the initial process that I underwent that gave me the gifts of being free from the need of physical food, came through the ascension networks. Downloaded from Serapis Bay, in the early 1990's, it was trialed by one group based in Australia, with various success. For some it was an easy conversion, for others not, yet all experienced an increase in their intuitive abilities. As those abilities expanded so did our contact with and understanding of inter-dimensional life.

Q: Is knowledge or experience of these Beings of Light an important reality in The Prana Program?

A: No, for example – to use television venacular – some people only like the Buddhist or Muslem Cosmic TV channels and never channel surf, hence their experience of inter-dimensional realities remains vague or limited by choice. Others confine their dimensional experience to 3D Earth and its games of struggle for survival. Everything is possible and if we can think of something it can be brought into reality on some level or else we wouldn't have the thought. Hence we can access many of the benefits of The Prana Program using the science of the fields. Other benefits that are literally quite delightful – like liasing with inter-dimensional life – can only be enjoyed when we open to its channel. As creative beings we can choose to dwell in any reality we desire but choices are broadened with education and experience.

Q: You often say that human evolution and The Prana Program particularly, is being overshadowed by inter-dimensional Being's of great light and love, can you share more of this?

A: In my experiential model of reality, there are many inter-dimensional groups tuning into Earth's evolutionary process, guiding and overshadowing and sometimes interfering e.g. A recent TV series director Steven Spielberg called "Taken" focused a lot on interference by the Zeta Reticuli and their experimentations. However there are also benevolent bodies who download to open minds – via the U.F.I. – lots of evolutionary enhancing technology to guide Earth; from The Prana Program to Tesla technology, free energy systems and so much more.

Q: But didn't The Prana Program's nutritional aspect originally came from ancient wisdom sources not inter-dimensional?

A: All wisdom – at some point – is downloaded interdimensionally through the act of consciousness expansion that allows an individual greater access to the U.F.I., the Universal Field of Infinite Love and Intelligence.

Q: *For many years you promoted the Luscious Lifestyles Program as a way of increasing the pranic flow. How did you discover this?*

A: An eight point action plan that includes daily meditation, prayer, mind mastery, a light diet, exercise, service, time in silence and the use of mantras and devotional songs, these points formed the lifestyle that I found to be practiced by everyone who was experiencing the most benefits of The Prana Program. It is also the lifestyle that I received telepathically from Mother Mary when I asked her for a recipe to eliminate suffering on Earth.

Q: *In some very religious countries you are criticized more for your work with inter-dimensional life than for The Prana Program, why do you think this is?*

A: Religion and power often go hand in hand with many promoting that inter-dimensional contact is only possible through intermediaries such as gurus or priests. However in my reality and experience it is our calibration that determines contact with the Holy Ones and/or Angelics. Many power mongers do not like to hear someone say that God is within and that we can go direct to Source for anything as it shifts the balance of power and eliminates the need for middlemen.

Q: *You describe the path as that of the warrior and the goddess. The discipline of the warrior is clear; but what about the goddess and the Madonna Frequency?*

A: On one level living a prana only nourishment regime is a warrior path and it's not in everyone's blueprint to do it. To do it we need to be in balance which requires a blending of all the energies – masculine and feminine. But being in balance means different things to different people. When I was doing the research for the Light Ambassadry and going through that experience myself, I was attracted to and needed, the disciplined warrior energy.

Now that the foundation of our work has been laid, the energy has changed again to express more of the Goddess as the Divine Mother so my focus has shifted over the years to the benefits of manifesting Divine Love, within us and around us, and to the experience of Grace that this attracts. It is also the Goddess energy as the Madonna Frequency that is now beaming through inter-dimensionally to stabilize our world into a more peaceful expression.

༅ 3 ༅

Preparation, Physical Changes & Pre-programming

Q: What do you mean by "learning to listen to the voice of the body, and the need to develop a strong mind/body connection", in preparation for The Prana Program?

A: This is one of the first requirements and it means accepting and experiencing that:-

a) the body is perfectly capable of telling us exactly what it needs. Even if it is suffering ill health or disease, it can tell us exactly what steps we need to heal it. We can access its voice intuitively on a day to day basis, and also by using a system similar to kinesiology, such as the tools we offer in the Comfortable Conversion chapter.

b) Secondly, a strong mind/body connection means experientially understanding that every cell of the physical system is constantly attuned to our thoughts and understanding the effect this has on the body via a process of thought experimentation e.g. thought monitoring where we see the benefits of positive thinking.

Both of these are important in experiencing all the benefits of The Prana Program.

Q: You also insist that people learn to hear and listen to and adopt the guidance of the Divine One Within them – their DOW – and that this is also crucial in the preparation process. Why?

A: As we are all unique, there is no one way to increase the pranic flow to experience all its benefits. Our personal field of resonance determines the cosmic particle magnetic process and this field is influenced by our environment, genetic line and also past experiences, plus the mindsets and perceptions formed by all of these. Hence the only one who has all the answers for us is our DOW as it is immortal and all knowing in nature and has no information or guidance restrictions. If we can formulate the question, the answers will come. How our body responds and what it needs to maintain perfect health and nutritional levels, in The Prana Program, can only come from this inner voice of intuition for only its intimate knowledge of our bio-system can provide all the insights and answers.

Q: You always say that a person needs to adopt certain mindsets with the prana program and engage in mind mastery, can you elaborate on this?

THE PRANA PROGRAM
Enjoyable & Effective Evolution with Jasmuheen
e-book at http://www.selfempowermentacademy.com.au/htm/cia-education.asp#pranaprogram

A: Our beliefs and self talk constantly affect both brain and cellular operation and hence certain mental attitudes and mindsets need to be understood and adopted in order to begin to be nourished by prana. Once we understand what prana is, and how it can feed us, then we need to expect it to. For successful pranic nourishment an attitude that:-

"All my nourishment, all my vitamins, all my minerals, everything I need to maintain a healthy body, comes from prana" is step one.

Next an attitude that "I only eat for pleasure, not for need as prana provides all I require" is another new mindset. Both commands help to rewire the brain's neural pathways.

Q: Can you explain what you mean by the phrase "I only eat for pleasure, not for need."?

A: Firstly as mentioned this statement begins to reprogram the neural pathways in the brain. Secondly the statement accepts the possibility thus making it more real. An earlier survey found that 73% of people who do the 21 day process eventually go back to eating while the statistics for The Food of Gods prana program are a lot less. This happens because once you know you don't need food and have proven it by doing it then you have a choice. This is a great freedom – to not need food and to lose the attachment to it, and to randomly eat for pleasure only rather than regularly for need, which in turn has a huge impact on our consumption of global food resources.

Q: Many people say that increasing the pranic flow through their system also increases their sensitivity, often making them feel overwhelmed by denser energies in the world. Why does this occur and how can they combat this?

A: This occurs because we are in "unconscious absorption" mode, meaning we are too aware of, and sensitive to, what is around us and we allow it all to infiltrate our auric field and often drain and/or overwhelm us. Consequently we need to switch into a mindset where we only radiate rather than absorb. We do this by plugging into a limitless source of love, wisdom and power within us, and then we intentionally radiate this mix of energy through us, from the inner planes and out into the world. We can also cocoon ourselves in a field of violet light and utilize some of the bioshield devices we share of in detail in *The Food of Gods* manual.

Q: How does one become a pranic nourisher and increase the pranic flow? What prerequisites are there?

A: To do this successfully an individual needs to be a tuned instrument who practices mind mastery – that is conscious re-programming for the elimination of any limiting and non-honoring beliefs. By non-honoring, I mean maintaining beliefs that do not recognize the glory of the DOW and its gift of our life. We also need to recalibrate our personal field of resonance to specific frequencies in order to attract enough cosmic particles to nourish us in a healthy way. Other prerequisites for being a pranic nourisher would simply be the heartfelt desire to be limitless and to live life to the highest maximum potential in a way that is harmonious to others. This is about honoring ourselves enough to open-mindedly explore exciting possibilities, to be passionate about being alive, to maintain a heart filled with joy and gratitude at the gift we have been given to simultaneously create, and also witness the majesty of creation. This mindset also increases the cosmic fire aspect of cosmic particle flow. Cosmic fire is Divine Love.

For some this also means to be able to absorb all that we desire, from all dimensions, through these five physical senses. As we shared earlier, increasing the pranic flow also requires us to utilize our two more refined senses of intuition and knowing by activating and stimulating the master glands in our body that govern these – the pituitary and pineal.

Q: What specific physical changes have you personally noticed?

A: My stomach has shrunk, my metabolic rate has slowed, until I started 'nibbling' – to fulfill my interest in flavor – I never got hungry. I need a lot less sleep, my mental clarity has improved, I have become more detached emotionally, I feel very 'light', vaster, more multi-dimensional somehow. Sometimes – when walking – I have felt that the only reason I know I'm physical is by my footsteps and shadow but this was only in the initial stages and as time goes by we become more grounded and integrated. Some of these things may be due to the current energy influxes on the planet also affecting many. In the first few months of the transition I also experienced a little extra hair loss when washing and brushing my hair which others have also reported. This is only temporary and settles down to 'normal' in a month or so.

Q: You often state, that it can take a bio-system 6-9 months to adjust to the prana only nourishment aspect of the program. Why?

A: Again this depends on an individual's calibration which we will look at in detail in the next chapter. However, my research has found that while energy levels are high, things like weight stabilization can often take between 6-9 months so we need to have patience and give the program the time it needs for fine-tuning and adjustments.

Q: So how do you sustain body weight once you are on a prana only nourishment?

A: Through re-programming the body and a strong mind/body connection, plus having trust and faith that is also based on re-education into understanding how the body operates when we increase the pranic flow and act as masters of the vehicle.

The idea that one has to lose weight and/or die, if we do not eat food, is simply that – a belief. Society tells us we need a balanced diet, vitamins etc. to be healthy and, because of their belief systems, for the general population this is true. Being sustained by prana has more to do with our spiritual journey and awakening, a consequence of such is that we can be sustained by light and love of our DOW which has the ability to mainfest all that we need on all levels.

The physical body is the servant to the mental body which when aligned serves the spiritual body. By changing our beliefs and mindset we can simply program ourselves to maintain a desired weight and we will. Every cell of our body constantly hears our self-talk and if our self-talk is limiting then the cell behaves in a limiting manner.

I also recommend that people do not weigh themselves as they transition through this change, as even thoughts such as "Oh no I weigh only _____!" can upset the new programming patterns we are laying into the system.

In India today there are yogis with such command over their molecular structure that they can be buried alive for weeks at a time, or drink poison with both having no negative physical affects. They achieve this due to their high levels of self mastery over their physical, emotional and mental systems. Studies have also researched the benefits of intention regarding placebo medicine.

Q: Post conversion, why can some people stabilize their weight quickly and others can't?
A: Our research has shown that this depends on individual mind mastery and/or also the strength of past cellular memory influences and personal calibration levels.

Q: How come some people lose no weight when they convert to The Prana Program?
A: This is due to the fact that they are already calibrating at the level to attract the perfect flow of cosmic particles that they need to feed them and have usually been minimalistic in their physical diet before conversion, for example, one small meal a day of non-fattening type food e.g. fruit or raw vegetables combined with a mindset that all vitamins etcetera come from prana.

Q: How can people also put on weight when they are not eating physical food?
A: Strangely the energy of love can feed us and as we increase this flow of love through our system it can increase our weight unless we redirect the excess energy into the world through selfless service.

Obviously giving and receiving keeps an energetic balance, while just receiving and storing creates excess.

Q: What are your personal energy levels like, do you ever feel tired?
A: Rarely, of course this depends on how much I do. As my creativity levels have increased so much, I always have to be aware of balance and make sure that I spend time doing all the things that I love that keep my passion for life strong. Lack of passion for life can drain us as can choosing toxic ways of being.

Q: Do you need as much sleep?
A: As I find that my energy levels are consistently high with lack of energy being an absolute rarity, I find I can easily attend to my work/service commitments often for up to 20 hours per day before feeling any desire for sleep. One thing I have noticed is that my ability to be without sleep is dependant upon the 'type of energy' I am tuning to at the time. If I am 'working' and consciously plugged into what I call the cosmic service circuit board then I am so energized that I feel a vastly decreased need for sleep.

Q: What about dreamtime, don't people miss this if they rarely sleep and does an individual's lucid dreaming abilities increase with The Prana Program?
A: Yes and yes.

Sometimes pranic nourishers may stimulate the digestive system into action – via the ingestion of food – just so that they can feel tired and sleep to dream.

Lucid dreaming abilities increase naturally as we decrease our physical, emotional and mental toxicity levels but self training in this field also helps.

Q: What about physical body elimination, urination and defaecation?
A: This depends on the personal program, some individuals who are nourished by prana have one small meal once a month for social reasons, others one small meal once a week, others live only on liquids which may include light soups, coffee, tea (which they transmute into a frequency beneficial for their body), others have mainly water with a fruit juice now and then for flavor. How much they ingest in addition to obtaining nourishment from prana then determines how much they will eliminate.

It also depends on if we are living in a highly polluted external environment like a busy city or if we are living in a purer atmosphere such as the beach or mountains where there is a high prana content in the air and surrounds.

It is said, via some research sources, that we can absorb up to two litres of water a day through the pores of our skin via literally drinking from the atmosphere, so even for the true breatharian who neither eats nor drinks, they still obtain external moisture in this way and will hence continue to urinate.

When I was taking a maximum of three small glasses of liquid each day I found myself eliminating fluid and approximately every three weeks what I call 'rabbit droppings' which for me was uncomfortable. I was intuitively advised that, as I lived in a city, pollutants and dead cells would allow this to continue. I later found that taking a small amount of prune juice once a week made this small elimination more comfortable.

Q: What role does physical exercise play in The Prana Program? Why do you always encourage people to build muscle strength?
A: Basically a strong system can attract, hold and radiate more potent frequencies. Building muscle mass aids this so I always recommend a training program that improves both strength and flexibility. Ashtanga-Yoga/weight lifting, dance or whatever else a person is drawn to. Walking in highly pranic environments such as at the beach or mountains is also beneficial.

Q: What about menstruation?
A: It is said that woman are born with a certain number of eggs for fertilization so if a body is healthy and being nourished then menstruation will continue until all eggs are released. If a woman is receiving enough prana to keep her healthy then she will continue to menstruate until it is her natural time not to.

Q: Do you take vitamins?
A: No. One of the first things I realized was that I had to let go of the idea that anything other than prana would nourish me. If I was to change my mindset and totally trust that prana alone could sustain me then I could not take vitamins as there would be no need. This was a hard one for me as having been a vegetarian for over 20 years prior to my pure prana diet conversion, I had always taken vitamins, particularly spirulina and B12. If you trust prana to sustain and regenerate the body and align to its channel so that it can, then it will.

After discovering the body's need for good nutrition and vitamins, which is a must when we stay anchored in a brain wave pattern, it is wonderful to know that when we anchor ourselves in the Theta-Delta realm, that the body can access its nourishment differently and hence eliminate our need for vitamins and minerals through physical food or supplements. This alone is very freeing and financially beneficial as prana is free and available to all.

Q: What about if someone is on medication – is it safe for them to live on a prana only nourishment?

A: This is something that only their DOW can guide them with. Anyone doing this needs a strong mind/body connection and to trust and hear the guidance of their DOW.

Q: What has been your biggest challenge with this prana process and its aspect of no longer needing physical food?

A: For me I would have to say my challenge has been with a lingering desire for flavor and also having to deal with my blueprint of being public with this research. The physical body, due to my background, has been relatively easy to master. With my European upbringing and its social emphasis on food and sharing, dealing with the emotional attachment to food has been less easy. One only has to look at what and when people eat to see that 90% of eating is based on emotional issues, even social dining is both physically and emotionally driven.

Mastering the mental body has been the most difficult. And with any prolonged 'fast' the senses become enormously heightened – the sense of smell, touch, hearing, sight and taste, all of these are naturally satisfied in living, yet when one ceases to eat or taste, the sense of flavor is then ignored so this can take adjustment.

Others on this path have mixed up all sorts of flavorsome drinks to satisfy their desire for flavor. As I initially stayed mainly with water and tea and held the desire to move beyond the consciousness of food, then over time the desire for flavor variety became more of an issue for me and one I still indulge from time to time.

Q: If we choose to no longer eat and let prana nourish us, are there other ways to satisfy our desire for taste?

A: The Ayurvedic tradition offers a wonderful range of herbs and spices to totally satisfy all our taste desires, herbs which can be steeped in hot water and drunk like tea. This vedic science of healing also links our taste buds and organs and some have begun to do further research on this connection. Also we have found that aromatherapy is a very powerful way of satisfying our sense of taste by using smell instead as many oils when smelt will alleviate an individual's desire for flavor.

Q: How beneficial are lifestyle tools, such as meditation and gradual dietary refinement, for the conversion to a pure prana nourishment stream?

A: The greatest source of physical, emotional, mental and spiritual nourishment comes via our day to day lifestyle and how we choose to spend our time as we keep repeating. Creating physical health, fitness and strength depends on a number of factors and much research has already been done in this field, for example we know that drinking pure water, eating fresh healthy food – preferably vegetarian, exercising regularly and engaging in meditation to deal with mental and emotional stress, are all extremely good for us.

We also know as metaphysicians that time spent in silence in nature and that exercising self mastery and mind control via re and de-programming our bio-system, is also beneficial in the creation of mental and emotional health, as is the use of devotional music or chanting and mantras. Add daily selfless service and prayer and we have a basic health and happiness lifestyle recipe that will help us tune to the perfect frequency field to eventually enjoy all of The Prana Program benefits. We share of this lifestyle in detail in my book, *Four Body Fitness – Biofields and Bliss*.

Q: You always say that success for a pure prana diet depends on personal resonance, what do you mean by this?

A: As mentioned already, personal resonance is a result of our lifestyles and how we choose to spend our time which influences the type of frequencies we transmit into the universal and global fields. Being in balance, being lovingly aware of self and others, living a life where we are listening to our intuitive voice, all of this affects our personal field of resonance and in turn how the universal field responds to us. The type of frequencies we transmit then determine the level of cosmic particles or chi that we can attract, hold, utilize and radiate. Thus we become a person who can feed ourselves internally by this flow and also feed the world by our Presence due to what we are radiating.

I would like to add that one of the main keys to access the Theta-Delta field of pure prana is our purity of heart. This means that our emotional field needs to pulse with the signals of sincerity, humility, surrender and compassion – things that cannot be taught except in the class called 'life' and via our interaction with living beings.

Q: You always say that people need to be in integrity in The Prana Program and also not expect to be popular or supported with this choice. Can you explain what you mean by this?

A: A person who acts with integrity will always be free of regret, especially when they act with a purity of heart and a desire to deliver something that is beneficial for all. Yet this will not shield the pure of heart from the anger, ignorance or confusion of those who will be challenged by a different view. So it is, and so it has always been, and so perhaps it will remain. And so it is that the information contained in <u>The Divine Nutrition Series</u> has, and will, challenge many industries from the medical and pharmaceutical to even the holistic health industry – as when we really tap into this field of nourishment all dis-ease and disharmony disappears so many practitioners in these fields will find the need for their services lessening. This threat of great change that our research offers is enough for many to prefer to negate its truth.

Q: How beneficial are colonic irrigations for detoxifying the system and readying it for a pure prana diet?

A: Keeping our bio-system clear of all toxicity – whether it is on physical, emotional, mental or spiritual levels is always beneficial, yet it is easier to do when we are well educated as to how to do this. If we have created high levels of toxicity due to dietary choices and attitudes then we can cleanse the system in many ways. A change in diet, using colonic irrigations to rebalance and stimulate a sluggish elimination system, as well as fasting, all of this has its place and needs to be undertaken if it feels right personally and is required by the body. Remember the body has its own voice that needs to be intuitively heard and listened to.

Q: Is it helpful to experience normal fasting before attempting a prana only regime?

A: Most definitely. Fasting and abstaining from food has many beneficial effects and with The Prana Program it not only helps in preparation, as far as detoxification goes, but also helps to decrease our emotional dependence on a variety of flavors and gives us insight into social reaction and new behaviour patterns that occur when one fasts and abstains from socializing around the sharing of physical food. Fasting intermittently can also acclimatize us to social reactions and can teach us new ways of interacting socially.

Q: What else can you tell us about fasting?

A: The Encyclopaedia Britannica says fasting is "abstinence from food or drink, or both, for ritualistic, mythical, ascetic or other religious and/or ethical purposes. The abstention may be complete or partial, lengthy or of short duration. Fasting has been practiced from antiquity worldwide by the founders and followers of many religions, by culturally designated individuals (e.g. hunters, or candidates for initiation rites) ...

"In the religions of ancient peoples and civilizations, fasting was a practice to prepare persons, especially priests and priestesses, to approach the Deities. In the Hellenistic mystery religions (e.g. the healing cult of the God Asclepius) the Gods were thought to reveal their divine teachings in dreams and visions only after a fast that required the total dedication of the devotee ... In the religions of traditional or preliterate peoples, fasting is often practiced before or during a vision (e.g. among the North American Indian peoples of the great plains of the Pacific North West). Among the Evenk (Tungus) of Siberia, Shamans (religious persona thought to have the power to heal and to communicate psychically) often received their initial visions not with a quest but rather after an unexplained illness; after the vision however, they fast and train themselves to see future visions and to control spirits."

Research goes on to share how:- "Fasting and spiritual mastery have gone hand in hand throughout time – from the Pueblo Indians of Americas South West, to Jainism where fasting is done according to certain prescribed rules using specific meditations, that bring on trance and heightened awareness.

"In the Therovada School, Buddhists fast on holy days and Sadhus (Holy men) in India are known to frequently fast. In the west, Judaism, Christianity and Islam also emphasize fasting during certain periods – Yom Kippur, Lent, Ramadan are all times of fasting and abstinence for many due to their religious ideologies and rituals." Even Mother Mary in her visits to places such as Fatima, has talked about the power of prayer and fasting.

Q: You have spoken of the benefits of a prana only nourishment, so what are some of the physical changes that can occur within a person when they allow pure prana to nourish them?

A: Some changes are as follows:- our stomach shrinks, our metabolic rate changes, we get more energy as prana is a purer source e.g. no chemicals, we sleep less, get stronger, never feel hungry as we are fed on a different level that also takes care of our physical, emotional, mental and spiritual hungers, our eyes light up to reflect a happier soul, and our pituitary and pineal glands also often light up and become brighter.

Q: Can we use testing methods like kinesiology, to determine the percentage we are being fed by prana as part of the prepatory process?

A: Yes, according to David Hawkins's research in his book *Power vs. Force,* there are many things we can discern about the way our physical system is currently operating. There are also other methods of discerning information from our body that I will share of – along with more on David's work – in the next section. We will also provide questions for you to find answers to regarding conversion to The Prana Program and checking your current status within it.

Q: What about preparation for physical immortality?

A: As I travel I find that more and more people are discovering that their blueprints contain the natural pre-programmed interest and ability to learn and demonstrate physical immortality. Our research has found that to do this successfully we need to:-

1) let go of limiting belief systems and all fear of physical death;
2) release restrictive mortality patterns;
3) reprogram the master glands of the systems;
4) act as if it is possible and a truth for us;
5) repattern our self-talk into the "I have forever" reality of an immortalist.

For an indepth article/s on this go to
http://www.selfempowermentacademy.com.au/htm/divine.asp

Q: Does the aging process automatically stop with pranic nourishment?

A: Not necessarily as this depends on mind talk and what type of hormones our master glands are releasing as they can either produce the death hormone or life sustaining hormones. What they produce is a mirror of our beliefs.

Q: Is stopping the aging process just a matter of increasing the pranic flow?

A: No we need to also work on mental attitudes. We also need to reprogram our master gland function to change the hormonal flow through the endocrine system which is the bio-system bridge between the physical and non-physical world.

Q: How do we stop the aging process of the body?

A: Similarily to the above in the preparation for physical immortality question – with particular focus regarding self-talk and also re-programming our master glands hormone production. Many people are unaware of how much damage limiting self-talk does to the human body, and how well it responds to limitless thinking, and how beneficial commands such as, "I am younger and younger everyday" are. Again the exact tools for this are provided in *The Food of Gods* and *The Law of Love* e-books.

Q: You suggest ordinary people can master techniques for halting death and decay; but doesn't that take years or lifetimes?

A: Who is to say that the man in the street wasn't a yogi in his past life? If you have had training in other lifetimes and have maintained that calibration then some can click right into it very easily. Who are we to say that someone is ordinary or unaware? They may have had amazing esoteric training in another life and be completing other seemingly more mundane assignments this life, so that when they get this information it triggers something and they switch into a different way of being. But yes, this is an initiation that has taken a long time for people to train for successfully. Many go through the prana conversion process that I talk of in the first book, but are unable to sustain the prana only lifestyle choice because their resonance does not attract a strong enough stream of cosmic particles from either the inner or outer planes. It can also be a challenge for those who miss the pleasure of eating.

Q: You used to talk a lot about the need to be physically, emotionally, mentally and spiritually fit in order to successfully live on a prana only nourishment, these days you focus more on calibration. Why?

A: While we will discuss calibration in detail in the next chapter, calibration is simply a proven safe way of measuring how prepared we are for this program, as it is a clear indication and confirmation of our fitness levels, so both are relevant.

Q: Is the pranic nourishment that you practice based in Kriya-Yoga, as Yogananda describes in his book Autobiography of a Yogi?

A: In this work we are all tapping into the same blueprint, a matrix some call Universal Mind, which holds data like in a 'cosmic computer bank'. I assume that Yogananda also received 'downloads' of information from this field as in essence we are all talking about the same thing and although one doesn't need to do Kriya-Yoga to live on light, I personally feel that pranic breathing helps. Our work is based on the premise that even though we're all everyday people, we're also all divine instruments and we can consciously tune ourselves and have experiences which some people might term miraculous.

Q: How beneficial is yogic training for being a prana nourisher?

A: As Yoga has become so popular in our western world, it is good to understand the different types of yogic practice and how they relate to pranic feeding. Firstly it is virtually impossible to provide a specific Divine Nutrition access procedure for as we keep stressing, it is all to do with our individual frequency which is determined by our past and present experiences and attitudes, and no two individuals are the same. However we can provide a selection of tools for tuning to the Divine Nutrition prana channel so that the individual can then experiment with this and yogic practice is one of these tools.

Q: You mention both Kriya-Yoga and Surya-Yoga; can you explain the difference and their benefits?

A: Mikhael Aivanhov shares in his Surya-Yoga book: "by focusing all his powers of concentration on the sun, he (an esoteric student) can capture and draw into himself, in all their original purity, the elements needed to ensure his health and equilibrium". He also says that as the sun provides all the elements for all life, we can feed on its pure essence and that: "If you want to be like the sun, you must gaze at it with great love and trust. In this way you will become warmer and more luminous and better able to pour life into others. Your presence among others will be that of a sun radiating light, warmth and life."

As we discussed in our previous books, the most prolific modern day research into pranic nourishment was done in India at the turn of the millennium with Dr Shah and his team and their 'guinea pig' Hira Ratan Manek – a yogi also known as Shri HRM. However Surya-Yoga involves more than solar gazing and absorbing the pranic flow through nature. Surya-Yoga incorporates all the other yogic practices while focusing on connecting with the Supreme Intelligence that feeds our physical sun and flows through it and recognizing the Divine Force that sustains our sun and directs its energy into the lower dimensions.

While Surya-Yoga is yoga of the sun, the practice of Kriya-Yoga is the yoga most adopted by many previous pranic nourishers, for Kriya-Yoga is the yoga of Light and its range of color. It consists of thinking on light, visualizing light and experiencing the inner Light flow via yogic practice, working with light energy through our auric field and learning to direct this light flow in a nourishing way as per practices like the Tao Master's Microcosmic Orbit.

It was a specific Kriya-yogic practice that sustained Giri Bala enough to be free from the need of food or fluid for over six decades and Kriya-Yoga that gave the Himalayan Babaji his immortality. Kriya-Yoga also feeds our chakras and their associated meridians.

The website: http://www.kriyayoga.com provides details on the Metaphysical Physiology of Kriya Pranayama. Here they say: "Kriya Yoga is called a 'scientific method of self-realization'.

Scientific, because it can be practiced by anyone and if properly done, everyone will achieve the exactly same results: God-union and self-realization.

"Devotion to God, Love for God, opens the door to Divine energy, bliss entering through your soul into your spiritual body – even purging into your physical body and providing you with health and strength. But that is just a side-effect of Kriya Yoga never the purpose of it."

Q: Can you explain a little more about other types of yogic practice and their preparatory relevance to The Prana Program?
A: Yoga is a metaphysical art that comes from India and Tibet, China, Japan, Egypt and also Persia and all religions have their own form of yoga. For example the practice of adoration, prayer, contemplation and devotion to God in Christianity is known as Bhakti-Yoga in India. Without devotion to our DOW and our desire to feel Its love, we cannot begin to connect to the Divine Nutrition prana channel, for devotion to the experience of Divine Love attracts the food of the Gods.

All recognized organisms including mankind are fed by the energy that radiates through our physical sun. To practice Hatha-Yoga and its various asanas in the warmth of the early morning or dusk time sun, opens and feeds all our meridians and our chakra system with another level of food and power. Applying positive mental projections and thought forms with Mantra-Yoga and using Kriya-Yoga to direct the outer light flow into our inner system, allows our sun time of Surya-Yoga to be even more beneficial.

Using Mantra-Yoga to remind us that the sun is also the Source of nourishment for all life, we can then change our mindset by acknowledging that it has the power to feed us directly without going through the middle man food chain of the plant and animal kingdom.

Q: You also often recommend the practice of Ashtanga-Yoga and also Laughter-Yoga. Why?
A: Ashtanga-Yoga uses our own body weight to build strength, flexibility and muscle mass so it is a valuable tool in allowing us to attract, hold and radiate more cosmic particles. Together with the practice of Kriya-Yoga, Surya-Yoga and Bhakti-Yoga we can tune ourselves very powerfully to enjoy more of the prana channel. Laughter-Yoga is beneficial to all our organs and keeps us healthy and in the perfect space to enjoy life. The more we laugh and love the more laughter and love we attract.

Q: Apart from yoga, is there any other form of exercise that you recommend, i.e. something that you personally do to maximize the pranic flow?

A: Definitely, though what I am about to recommend is not possible for everyone, however for those living in open spaces like mountains and beaches it is wonderful.

Barefoot backward walking.

Some of the benefits of this are as follows:-

- ☺ Realigns hips, spinal column, muscular and bone structure.
- ☺ As you are walking backwards and cannot see where you are going, your conscious mind is removed and only intuition guides you. This stimulates right brain activity and rebalances the internal energy flow.
- ☺ It is a fantastic exercise for absorbing prana through the soles of the feet and also through the auric field especially when done barefoot and in a highly charged prana environment such as on a long stretch of beach or mountain/country setting.
- ☺ Firms gluteus maximus, medius and minimus (bottom) muscles and also quadriceps and hamstrings (biceps femoris muscle [long head], semitendenosus muscle, semimembranosus muscle, gracilis muscle, adductor magnus muscle, sartorius muscle, biceps femoris muscle [short head], iliotibial tract).
- ☺ Stimulates acupressure points in the toes that relate to the brain and so alters brain wave patterns.

*Q: **What is the simplest and most effective preparation for The Prana Program to receive it maximum benefits?***

A: Focus on your calibration as this is something that can be measured and forms a good safety model as per the data outlined in the next section. We recalibrate ourselves via our lifestyle so I recommend the adoption and practice of the 8 points in the Luscious Lifestyle Program as discussed at http://www.selfempowermentacademy.com.au/htm/library.asp#llp. This lifestyle will tune you physically, emotionally, mentally and spiritually so that you can increase your natural attraction levels of prana. Add to this a sincere heart filled with love for life and appreciation of life and we become well tuned to receive The Prana Program benefits.

*Q: **In** The Foods of Gods **manual you recommend a five step program of preparation, can you touch on these briefly here?***

A: Yes. In summary for those who are sincerely interested in the Divine Nutrition or Prana program we recommend the following:-

THE PRANA PROGRAM
Enjoyable & Effective Evolution with Jasmuheen
e-book at http://www.selfempowermentacademy.com.au/htm/cia-education.asp#pranaprogram

1. Practice the Luscious Lifestyles Program (L.L.P.) 8 point plan of daily meditation, prayer, programming and conscious mind mastery, light diet, service, time in silence in nature and the use of devotional songs and music.
2. Next, do what is required to become fit on all levels. The L.L.P. lifestyle has the capacity to bring you into physical, emotional, mental and spiritual fitness and to provide perfect nourishment on all these levels.
3. Tell the Divine One Within (your DOW) to harmoniously bring your physical, emotional, mental and spiritual being into The Prana Program reality, with joy and ease and grace, so that you maintain perfect health. Your relationship with this aspect of yourself is crucial in enjoying all The Prana Program benefits.
4. Read everything you can on this subject so that you are well informed and can make intelligent decisions then test to see what is in your blueprint.
5. Your responsibility as someone being nourished by The Prana Program is to hold the vision that this gift of freedom will transform our world into a planet that dwells in a deep contented peace. Your holding of this vision will open an energetic doorway for this reality to move through and be anchored in the fields.

Most of all, having done the above points 1-5 we recommend that you relax and have some fun, be a great example, apply the minimum effort for maximum impact game and do it all with a smile. It is imperative that when seeking to be nourished solely by Divine Nutrition, that we all:-

1) act impeccably
2) act as masters and
3) hold the attitude that your physical, emotional, mental and spiritual bodies are here to serve you as a God in form.

Q: Although you never say you never eat, is it true that on average you have healthily lived on less than 300 calories per day for 12 years?

A: Yes. I would also like to add that many see The Prana Program as a black and white reality where people either eat (take physical food nourishment) or don't eat (live only on prana). This is not a reality that I like to promote as it is not that simple as there are so many factors influencing the way we are taught to nourish ourselves.

Nonetheless imagine the impact on resources if everyone could hook into the pranic flow to obtain their nourishment and only ever ate for pleasure rather than need? Imagine if we all could healthily exist on 300 calories per day? What impact would this have on resources? Imagine if we even adopted the Lama diet and lifestyle as per Peter Kelder's book *The Fountain of Youth*?

Q: Can you elaborate on the Lama lifestyle?

A: There are a group of Lamas in a monastry in the Himalayas who never appear to age. Looking eternally young, strong, fit and healthy, every day they meditate, chant, do physical labor, practice the five Tibetan rites and have only one meal a day of one type of food. Living on potato one day or carrots the next, they consume minimum amounts yet due to their lifestyle they calibrate at the perfect resonance to attract enough cosmic particles to maintain nutritional health. Even western research has shown that reducing our calorie intake can extend our lifespan although in metaphysical realities some say that our exact birth and death times are set.

PRE-PROGRAMMING & OTHER RESEARCH

Q: Do you think that certain people are attracted to this reality for a reason?

A: Over the years, due to my close interaction with many thousands of people, I have come to believe that those attracted to The Prana Program, and particularly its freedom from limitation aspects, are pre-programmed prior to their embodiment to be part of this wave of evolutionary change. Hence they feel it is something natural for them to experience personally and exhibit.

Q: You often talk about fulfilling blueprints we set for this life before our embodiment, what do you mean by this?

A: Simply that prior to embodiment, souls look at their prospective life and agree to fulfill certain things on both a personal and planetary level. This is called a blueprint or loose set of plans – which are the goals that we set. How we achieve these goals and the detail involved in doing so is a free will game that we design to both test and expand ourselves.

Q: If people are pre-programmed to do this then how do they find out? Is everyone's blueprint held in the Akashic records?

A: It's held in our lightbody. The Akashic records record the etheric imprints from our lifestyle choices. Every thought and action we choose is 'rubber-stamped' etherically in the quantum field, plus those things that have impact are stored within Universal Mind, the matrix called the Akashic records. The data as to our pre-programming can be accessed from cellular memory during deep meditation and we discuss how to access our pre-programming for The Prana Program in *The Food of Gods* (Meditation technique no.12 – Chapter 11).

THE PRANA PROGRAM
Enjoyable & Effective Evolution with Jasmuheen
e-book at http://www.selfempowermentacademy.com.au/htm/cia-education.asp#pranaprogram

Q: Can anyone access the Akashic records?

A: Yes. If we can think it, we can do it. Some say that the prophecies are about the collision of the worlds as the worlds of matter and spirit are bridging. In our work it is more like a very sweet transfiguration - at least that's what we wish to achieve. We all have a role to play with this and the Akashic records store all the data we need to do this. There is nothing new - wisdom is wisdom, it's not the revelation that is important, it's what we choose to do with it and how we choose to apply it. It's time to get practical and learn how to access and apply the wisdom we have within. The most powerful thing we can do is just ask our DOW for the answers and for the universe to reveal the realms of higher possibility in such a way that we are completely free from doubt. With doubt, we can't progress.

Q: Doesn't doubt need to be disproved in material reality?

A: yes and it's so easy to prove all this by sincerely asking the universal field to provide us with powerful experiences that will free us from all doubt, especially regarding our Divine essence and the power of Grace. Due to the nature of the pranic field, which is a field of loving intelligence that reveals itself when sought, all the forces gather to help us remember our true nature when we seek to re-experience it in a more conscious manner, especially when we seek to express this nature in a manner that is beneficial to our world. There are many ways for us to experience what were meant to in a way that frees us from doubt and sincerely asking is the first step.

Q: Can you share more on your own blueprint regarding anchoring The Prana Program in this world?

A: For me my role in The Prana Program has been as follows:-

1) Discover The Prana Program's gifts and live it all experientially thus proving to myself beyond a doubt its infinite possibilities as outlined in all of our books. This is a journey I intuitively began preparation for as a child.

2) Research all that I could on the subject, write about it and offer my research to the world in a pragmatic and simple way as possible. This included researching and simplifying data in the ancient and hidden mystery schools and personally undergoing various alchemical initiations.

3) Be a bridge regarding The Prana Program between the eastern understanding, and experience of prana, and introduce the benefits of increasing the pranic flow as widely as possible to the west in a way that supports the paradise agenda.

4) Find and support other proponents of this and introduce their methodologies through our networks.
5) Be a media spokesperson for The Prana Program and via holistic education principles utilize the media to anchor The Prana Program reality in the morphogenetic field.
6) Set up both innernet and internet communications systems to share our research en mass as per my constant touring and websites.
7) Introduce The Prana Program and its benefits through my political networks, and formulate an effective program to combine and share our research with existing aid and resource redistribution programs (if possible and if not to do it anyway).

Over the last decade we have achieved points 1 to 6 and are now completing point 7. It was not in my blueprint to give a year or two of my time – as Hira Ratan Manek has done – to personally be involved with extensive medical and scientific testing. Yet it was in my blueprint to act as a cosmic reporter and share the results of Hira's testing which has essentially proven the same thing – that a person can access enough prana, as an alternate form of nourishment so that they are free from the need to take physical food.

Summary

For me the best preparation process is to experiment and experience and then choose what allows you to feel and function best.

For example, I discovered in my early teens that my body's energy levels were greatly improved when I exercised regularly and had a light mainly raw-food diet. Later when I began meditation and yoga my bio-system functioned even better and the benefits were obvious. The process of physical, emotional, mental and spiritual refinement can bring incredible rewards that come through time, dedication and interest based on personal experimentation and via learning to listen to our inner voice and also the needs and voice of the physical body.

ॐ 4 ॐ

Calibration, Testing & Comfortable Conversions

Q: How is calibration different to personal frequency or resonance?

A: When we use the term calibration in The Prana Program we do so in context with the work done by David Hawkins and the system he developed and discusses in his book *Power vs. Force.* When we use lifestyle tools we can recalibrate our systems into emitting a different frequency and hence change universal field reaction to us. So calibration is a measurement of change in this context and is a way of both measuring and altering our resonance.

Q: During 2004 and 2005 you spoke a lot about personal calibration and safety levels for the pure prana, or true breatharian lifestyle, can you elaborate on this?

A: Yes our experience with the *Living on Light* book that offered the 21 day process was that 70% of people, converting to The Prana Program via that method, ignored the guidelines. This created safety problems in the conversion process so we offered a safer model in *The Food of Gods* manual. Shortly after this we came across David Hawkins's Kinesiology research and discovered we could apply his type of testing methods to verify people's readiness for a prana only nourishment hence making the conversion process even safer.

Q: Isn't living purely on prana safe?

A: Yes if we are well prepared, but for many it requires that they live a lifestyle like a spiritual athlete as per the 8 point Luscious Lifestyle Program already mentioned.

Q: What is kinesiology?

A: Founded by Dr George Goodheart and given wider application by Dr John Diamond, Behavioral Kinesiology is the well established science of muscle testing the body where a positive stimulus provokes a strong muscle response while a negative stimulus provokes a weak response. It is a way of talking to the body and getting clear responses as to its need and current capabilities.

Q: How does this apply to calibration?

A: Using Diamond's system, over a twenty year study period Hawkins developed "a calibrated scale of consciousness, in which the log of whole numbers from 1 to 1,000 determines the degree of power of all possible levels of human awareness". In this model 200 represents emotions of positive stimulus where muscle response remains strong and below 200 is where muscle response weakens as emotions such as anger, fear, guilt or shame, begin to influence and weaken the body.

In this model 200 is also the energy calibration of truth and integrity, 310 is the calibration for hope and optimism, 400 is the energy of reason and wisdom, 500 is the energy of love, 540 of joy, 600 is perfect peace and bliss and 700 to 1000 represents even higher levels of consciousness.

Hawkins sees the potential of kinesiology as "the 'wormhole' between two universes – the physical, and the mind and spirit – an interface between dimensions ... a tool to recover that lost connection with the higher reality and demonstrate it for all to see".

Q: How did you apply this research to The Prana Program?

A: Excited by the possibilities that his calibration system offered as far as a way of checking our prana program freedom models, I began to apply it during my October/November 2004 tour. Quickly recognizing that we can use this system as a base, to move into levels perhaps unexplored by David Hawkins, during this tour I took advantage of testing and confirming my findings with hundreds of special test subjects from four different countries – France, Italy, Germany and Switzerland.

In order to understand this model fully, I recommend that you read his book as the calibration testing system can be used for testing many things, including the consciousness of Presidents and world leaders and influential decision makers. It can also be adopted to test the effectiveness of Third World programmes and we will discuss these things more fully in that section of this book.

Q: You have since modified this testing system further, why?

A: Our research found problems with the kinesiological model such as the need to have someone else test us and also the fact that as Hawkins himself shares, the calibration of the individual testing you and the calibration of the questions can affect the answers. Hence I set out to discover other methods of reliable self testing which the U.F.I. (Universal Field of Infinite Intelligence) eventually delivered. We will share these two additional testing tools shortly.

Q: Can you share a little more about the U.F.I.?

A: While I share my understanding of the U.F.I. later in this chapter, Hawkins shares: "The individual human mind is like a computer terminal connected to a giant database. The database is human consciousness itself, of which our own cognizance is merely an individual expression, but with its roots in the common consciousness of all mankind. This database is the realm of genius; because to be human is to participate in the database, everyone, by virtue of his birth, has access to genius. The unlimited information contained in the database has now been shown to be readily available to anyone in a few seconds, at any time in any place. This is indeed an astonishing discovery, bearing the power to change lives, both individually and collectively, to a degree never yet anticipated.

"The database transcends time, space, and all limitations of individual consciousness. This distinguishes it as a unique tool for future research, and opens as yet undreamed-of areas for possible investigation." He is of course talking about accessing the universal field of intelligence which is within and around us all and holds the answers to all our questions.

Q: Using Hawkins's model what did you first discover with the groups you tested?

A: Among the thousands of people that we have tested, in some of the countries mentioned, first we found that:-

- ☺ 80% tested yes that it is part of their blueprint to create a disease free life.
- ☺ 70% tested yes that it was part of their blueprint to learn how to be free from taking nutrition through food and access it through feeding from the divine nourishment flow within.
- ☺ 18% tested yes for setting up the reality of being free from the need for fluid, this lifetime, by again allowing that divinely nutritional source of prana within them to hydrate their body quite perfectly without the need for external fluids.
- ☺ 40% tested yes that it was part of their pre-agreed service blueprint to demonstrate physical immortality;
- ☺ 15% tested yes for pre-agreeing to learn, and demonstrate, the art of dematerialization and rematerialization and
- ☺ 70% tested yes for developing the ability to stop the ageing process.

As you can see from these figures, the types of people that are attracted to The Prana Program's freedom agenda are a very particular group of a very specific resonance. Hence having a model that can ascertain our calibration level before we enter into the release of these types of limitation adds a very beneficial layer. I mention this data first as it is wonderful to test for this type of information before seeking to experience some of The Prana Program's additional benefits.

By first checking if it is in your blueprint and then checking when and/or if the bio-system is ready and able to sustain this, we then have a safe system to advise us. For people already receiving sufficient nourishment from physical food, to attempt to do this without the support of the right calibration is only asking for potential physical trouble. For people in Third World countries who are already experiencing physical system stress due to lack of nourishment it is a different matter and we will discuss this in the last chapter of this book.

Q: What are the levels for safe conversions to the pure prana program?

A: Using David Hawkins's calibration testing system with kinesiology, our groups discovered and verified the below levels. When we tested the below question we initially used two test subjects. We used kinesiology and David Hawkins's system, and then we confirmed this using an additional two testing tools, thus using a triple bind test (with metaphysical methods). These answers were then confirmed by approximately 500 additional test subjects in late 2004 and this is what we have noted:-

- ☺ In order to establish a disease free existence where there is no physical, emotional, mental and spiritual disease, a human bio-system needs to maintain a personal calibration of 635.
- ☺ For the creation of an ageing free system, where the ageing process is literally stopped, a human bio-system needs a minimum calibration of 637. Interestingly this is very close to the calibration of a disease free existence.
- ☺ In order to safely exist purely on a prana only flow for nourishment, and no longer need to take physical food, a human bio-system needs to calibrate at 668.
- ☺ In order to safely exist with the fluid free existence, and be hydrated only by cosmic particles, a human bio-system needs to calibrate at 777.
- ☺ The calibration for physical immortality for a human bio-system is 909.

To read more on this please go to:
http://www.selfempowermentacademy.com.au/htm/files/downloads/Post-Script-SafetyCalibrationModel.pdf

Q: Will or can these calibration figures change in the future?

A: Yes definitely. As the morphogenetic field changes, due to more holistic education programs, then the levels of energy to support this paradigm will strengthen and make the future field more nurturing and the pathways easier to adopt. We have witnessed this already over the last decade as people are no longer shocked by this potential reality and are much better informed due to our media work. As the field of the mass of humanity changes, then the hundredth monkey system kicks in to change these calibration levels. According to Hawkins, while 78% of people calibrate at less than 200, mass consciousness as a whole registers at 207 due the process of entrainment where 22% of people of higher calibration are dominating the field enough to shift it into the level of truth and integrity en mass.

Q: Is the calibration discussion what you mean when you say that the real role of The Prana Program has nothing to do with whether a person eats or not, but more to do with their potential to influence the field?

A: Yes, The Prana Program's main gift is to shift a person's calibration so that they can attract, hold and radiate more love and wisdom – which I believe is the food that everyone is hungry for – and to attract this to feed not just their own systems but also to radiate this love and wisdom out into the greater field to feed the masses.

When Hawkins' book was first published in 1995, his research shared that only 4% of the world's population calibrated at over 500, while in 2004 it was 6%; and in 1995 only 1 in 10 million calibrated at over 600. **Nonetheless a person calibrating at 300 has the enough DOW power radiation to energetically feed and influence 90,000 people; and at a calibration of 700 we can counterbalance the energy of, and feed energetically 700 million.** These figures confirm that if all we do is refine our personal calibration levels to radiate maximum DOW power. This in itself is a valuable service, for not only does it deliver us naturally into the freedom agenda but it will also allow our presence here to positively influence the world.

Q: Is there anything else that you tested people for with this model that has relevance here?

A: Yes another thing that we tested was to ask the body consciousness of each person at what weight their body would stabilize at once they entered in the food free, and then later the fluid free, existence. I felt that by asking the body consciousness this question this is another wonderful way to affirm our readiness. For example, a few years ago when I checked where my body weight would stabilize at with a fluid free existence I was told 45kg. For me intellectually and emotionally I rejected this simply because I felt that it was not good for me to look so skeletal and so I held off on my decision to go onto a fluid free existence. When testing this same question in 2004, I was told that my body could sustain a fluid free existence at 51kg because my calibration had changed over the last few years. This was a lot more acceptable for me and therefore makes the movement into this level of freedom far more attractive.

Hence if you get a confirmation from your body of a weight that you feel is unacceptable to you then the advice is to wait and increase your personal calibration levels before going into this additional level of freedom. You can also test to see how much you are currently being nourished by prana and hydrated by cosmic particles. Strangely many people find that their percentage of cosmic particle hydration is higher than their cosmic particle nourishment levels.

Q: What else did you test for regarding the preparation conversion process?

A: We also had the groups test their home field and work field calibration levels. It is important to have a field calibration in your home (and work if possible) of a minimum of 200 which is, as David Hawkins has shared, the beginning levels of operating in truth and integrity. The higher the home field calibration then obviously the more supportive the environment is for you to move into and maintain these levels of The Prana Program's freedom agenda and the more comfortable your conversion process will be.

Q: What exactly is The Prana Program's freedom agenda?

A: Simplistically it's the benefits that come, the freedom from human limitations that come, when a person substantially increases the pranic flow through their bio-systems. These are the type of benefits we discussed in chapter 2.

Q: Apart from daily lifestyle and mind mastery, what is the simplest way to increase calibration levels?

A: The quickest way, as we all know, to increase calibration levels is simply to love a lot in life, for love is one of the most powerful feeding mechanisms that we have, so to enjoy and match our calibration levels with our DOW is a great focus to have and works powerfully because our Divine essence is pure and limitless love.

Q: What do you feel is the single most important requirement for a safe physical conversion to the food/fluid free aspects of The Prana Program?

A: Clear and trustworthy intuitive DOW guidance and the perfect calibration level.

Q: Why?

A: Because through this conversion process an individual changes and experiences influences that no-one else has answers to. Each person is a composite of so many influences that can affect the success of our conversion process e.g. genetic, cultural, past life, plus our vast emotional imprinting and actual physical resonance. No-one can guide you through this but the one who knows all about you, on all levels, and that is your DOW. Once you have established clear communication, that you have proven to yourself that you can trust, then you also need to have the perfect calibration to attract a strong enough and consistent enough flow of cosmic particles to maintain health and happiness.

Q: In your book Harmonious Healing – The Immortals Way ***you offer various "DDT's" and toured teaching these tools throughout 2005. Why?***
A: DDT's is short for Dependable Discernment Tools and they allow us to ascertain information from our body, and also from our DOW, as to a wide range of questions we have in life. Everyone I meet loves to get, or is seeking to get, clear inner guidance.

Q: Can you explain what these tools are and why they are so important?
A: Yes we work with a three level system of DDT's. Briefly these are as follows:-

System 1: Guidance from our DOW – the Divine One Within – which is our inner voice. Generally this must always be our first method of testing in that it is the only reliable source of confirmation that is completely incorruptible. This level of communication comes via our sixth and seventh senses of intuition and knowing and needs to be, in my opinion, our first barometer of guidance in everything that we do in life.

System 2: The second level of testing is to use a system like the art of kinesiology to gain information confirmation by testing muscle responses in the body. Kinesiology, as many trained in this field know, has its limitations. Hence we often also use the sway tool and the tummy breath tool as per below.

System 3: The third level of testing that is a wonderful support system for us is to ask to receive clear confirmation from the universal field of intelligence which is all around us. The universal field of intelligence responds to our telepathic thought patterns when we have a strong desire for knowledge that supports our own evolutionary path in a positive way. It is the alchemist's library and freeway through life.

Q: Can you elaborate on the system 2 tools? I.e. the sway tool and the tummy breath tool?
A: These are briefly as follows:-

The Sway Tool:

Breathe deeply and relax.

Center yourself so that you are in a place of stillness and ask your DOW to express itself clearly, through your body, through this tool.

Ask It to move you forward with a 'yes' answer and sway you backwards for a 'no' answer.

You need to be completely relaxed and let the chi of your DOW move you and not over-ride this with your mind.

So when you are calm and breathing in a relaxed manner, test this tool by asking yourself something like, for example, "I am in a female body". If this is true you will find yourself being pulled, or swaying slightly forward. If it is false you will find yourself swaying backward.

Then you are ready to move on to ascertain other things, like the questions at the end of this chapter.

The Breath Test Tool or Tummy Test Tool:

This is my preferred level of system testing as it follows the smooth deep flow of the One who breathes us – our DOW.

Test:

Get relaxed and again ask for your DOW to clearly express Itself through the rhythm of your breath.

Think of a statement you want verified.

Chant it over and over as you have your right hand resting gently on your abdomen, and your left hand on your chest so you can detect more easily the change in your breathing rhythm.

When we are in alignment with our truth on an issue, our breathing gets deeper and deeper, dropping naturally down into our "tummy" area. When we are in a state of incongruence, or falsity on an issue, our breathing naturally becomes shallow or higher up into the chest or throat.

As you chant the statement be aware of whether your breathing is deep or shallow.

Q: You often recommend that when we use kinesiology that we ask the Divine One Within to confirm data, using the muscle testing system through the body, rather than asking the body's consciousness itself. Why?

A: Because there is a huge difference between the voice of our DOW and the voice of the body consciousness which sees everything through a very limited perspective. In all system 2 testing methods asking our DOW to express Itself, through the body movements, is essential.

Q: After more than a decade of experiential research what do you feel is the simplest way of converting a body to a pure prana lifestyle?

- ☺ The changing and finetuning of our calibration through our 8 point daily lifestyle program with particular focus on programming and service.
- ☺ The setting of specific attitudes and intentions – particularly regarding the bigger picture of harmonious evolution.
- ☺ The implementation of internal field feeding systems to magnetize more cosmic particles for food and hydration.
- ☺ The expansion of heart chakra/love energy using the Love Breath tool and selfless service.

Some Post Prana Program Conversion Questions:

Q: Are there any associated health risks/problems or deficiencies (iron, b12) with prana only nourishment?
A: As stated previously, the essence of life is prana which carries within us all the vitamins and nourishment that is required to maintain an immortal, self-regenerating physical body. A person would only experience health risks or problems if they do not change their cellular/mental belief systems and/or if their calibration levels are too low to magnetize enough prana to provide all they need to maintain health.

Q: Is there anyone you would not recommend the prana only nourishment to?
A: I personally would not recommend this journey to anyone who is not sincerely interested in this reality as it is a path that requires conscious refinement. For this practice to be successful without detrimental effects one must honor the intellect via research and release all limited beliefs and be prepared to refine their personal calibration levels which due to lack of education about the benefits of this, many people will not do. Unfortunately there is still a bit of a "give me a pill and just fix it" mentality in our western world which often walks with apathy and skepticism.

Q: Does the body undergo any physiological changes?
A: If one practices mind mastery with programming and intention, one can change their whole experience of life as a lot of the work we are doing is about activating then utilizing the four-fifths of the brain that houses higher consciousness. Generally speaking, many individuals are too busy caught up with 'lower mind' issues of survival in physical reality to explore their full human potential. Once we have mastered issues of survival we are then free to explore higher consciousness, via meditation and other ancient or alchemical practices. This type of conscious tuning then allows us to enjoy great freedom from many perceived limitations.

THE PRANA PROGRAM
Enjoyable & Effective Evolution with Jasmuheen
e-book at http://www.selfempowermentacademy.com.au/htm/cia-education.asp#pranaprogram

***

Q: When was the last time you were personally tested regarding your own health levels?

A: When I was in Russia in mid 2005, I was tested using advanced auric field readers that can also attest to the health of my organs and all body aspects, including chakras, and they found that my readings were strong, balanced and healthy on all levels.

Q: But didn't you also manifest a life threatening illness in late 2004? Why did this happen if increasing the pranic flow can move you beyond the creation of disease as you report?

A: We always teach what we have come to learn ourselves and I needed to understand how to 'uncreate' diseases and to also discover more of the Dependable Discernment Tools to share with others. Manifesting and clearing this in my own system gave me many gifts I needed and we cover this journey in the *Harmonious Healing & The Immortal's Way* e-book. To me it was a brilliant adventure that gave tremendous insights as I have long taught a preventative medicine program but had an incomplete understanding of how to help move someone out of the grip of a potentially fatal disease or how to clear powerful and limiting mortality patterns. Manifesting this disease in my own body gave me all the answers to these things.

Q: What happens to the digestive organs of people who no longer choose to take physical food, do they wither and die?

A: There is an inner 'diagnosis' of reading energy fields intuitively that is called scanning. When we go into the body and look, with a tuned inner vision, we witness a flow of energy, like a wave, magnetize to our body. This happens in response to our instruction and command to universal forces to be pranically fed and prana then flows in through the pores of the skin. It also flows into the atoms via internal feeding mechanisms that we create and program to absorb prana from the inner planes. This then flows as pure nourishment into the cells and organs making them stronger and healthier than when they are fed via the ingestion of physical food. Hence the digestive organs operate in a healthy state of suspended animation.

Q: But how can you be sure your organs are okay?

A: Many of us have had both traditional and non-traditional – alternative therapy – testing with positive results. One challenge with this is that many western practitioners have had no previous experience with individuals who are nourished purely by prana so they have no previous 'yardsticks' for comparison. Also, generally speaking, by the time one has tuned their fields to being able to be sustained only by prana we are generally no longer creating any dis-ease or discomfort in the energy bodies to warrant seeing 'therapists' or doctors and tend to scan our own systems intuitively instead.

Q: How can people scan or self diagnose energetically?

A: To self diagnose energetically, I recommend that the individual recall the memory of the lifetime where they were well trained and practiced in this refined art of energy work and command full conscious awareness of, and ease with, the practice of energy diagnosis. It is simply intuition tuned to, and connected with, Universal Mind which holds this knowledge. It can never be misused for we can only attract to ourselves a vibration that mirrors our own consciousness. Of course for this we need to have a strong mind/body connection and to have learnt to hear and trust the body's voice and to open up our inner sight. Scanning is a matter of being still and consciously moving through the body to 'see' its inner state and then trusting what is intuitively revealed.

Q: Post conversion, if we find ourselves suddenly sleeping a lot less what do you recommend?

A: Enjoy the extra time with activities that amuse you, as your body will sleep when and if it needs to. Do not fall into the trap of classifying yourself as an insomniac and/or take something to help you sleep. Instead fill your time with enjoyable activities such as meditation, yoga, reading, listening to music and other quiet night time activities. Keep your system free from physical, emotional and mental toxicity and your physical body will find its own sleep rhythm. Lastly just accept that pranic nourishers generally need less sleep.

Q: And if we find we are sleeping more?

A: Check your calibration and percentage of pranic flow. Also be aware of your energy levels during the day – if all of this is good then perhaps you are receiving extra dreamtime training which you can also confirm using the tools given. If the answer is not supportive then you may be in fasting mode and not getting a strong enough flow of cosmic particles. Again test to see as your body has the answers.

Q: After conversion to a prana only nourishment, what happens to the taste buds? Do you crave flavors or a variety of taste sensations?

A: The major stumbling block for many involved in this pioneering work has been still craving flavor and more varied taste sensations. It is important to not be in denial and, as we slowly release our emotional dependence on food, some may continue to indulge in the intermittent pleasure of taste. What we have found is that when people stop eating initially they desire either a spicy flavor or a very sweet flavor, or may fluctuate between the two. Having a mouthful of the desired flavor when the craving hits satisfies many while they utilize re-programming methods to move beyond the consciousness of food. Most hold the intention that this is a joyous journey and not one of denial.

Q: What happens to a person if they learn to be nourished purely by prana and then later they begin eating physical food again?
A: If we begin to eat again – having established the prana feeding mechanisms successfully – then any physical food we eat is stored as fat as the metabolic rate is too slow to deal with it and also the body does not require it. However, as some people decide to eat from time to time, not for nutritional need but purely for social reasons, then in order to combat the weight gain – as they will be fed from two sources – then they need to exercise more to burn off the additional calorie intake or else they seem to gain weight.

Q: Are there any other problems with going back to physical food?
A: The majority of people who explore this journey return to eating quite easily by easing their way back to more solid food first with liquids – like soup – then fruit and vegetables, and then a normal diet. The main reason people return to eating is again social pressure and from being tired of being different and socially drawing attention to themselves.

Please note that regardless of whether one returns to eating, success is achieved in that a new pattern of knowing has been anchored that comes from the experience that one can exist for months or years by pranic feeding. This knowing is then laid down into cellular memory and a subtle yet powerful level of freedom is attained as we have proven to ourselves – by doing it – that prana can nourish us and so we may only eat from time to time for pleasure.

Q: Does there come a time after the conversion, where it is virtually impossible to return to a more solid food diet again?
A: On one level yes. We can always retrain the body to take physical food but once hooked into the pure prana channel, any physical food ingested will be stored as fat as we have already shared. Also you reach a point where you feel that you just operate far more effectively on a "prana only nourishment regime", so it feels archaic and strange to take physical food for nutrition, so people generally just eat sporadically for pleasure.

Q: Are there any obese pranic nourishers?

A: Yes there are people who have maintained good body weight with this. One woman weighed 90kg pre-prana only nourishment and then stabilized at 72kg with a pure breatharian no food no fluid situation. As she is less than 160cm tall some may say she is 'fat', yet to her she feels fantastic. I have also meet people who have lost no weight with this. Also please note that there are people who have begun this journey with an intention to lose weight. As this is a sacred initiation for the spiritual warrior, they have not been able to maintain the program and have subsequently gone back to eating. One's intention needs to be pure and in integrity.

Q: Is dehydration a worry? What do pranic nourishers drink, just water or flavored liquids as well? What about caffeine, alcohol and other stimulants?

A: There are beings who choose to neither eat nor drink but the majority of western pranic nourishers still maintain the ritual of socializing over a 'cuppa' so as not to be completely socially alienated. The majority do not indulge in alcohol as they may feel it lowers the vibrational rate of the energy fields of the bodies, or they may utilize mind mastery and transmute all that goes into the body into light. I personally still enjoy a good cup of tea!

Q: How do you transmute substances like coffee for example so that it is a frequency beneficial for the body?

A: This is done by will and intention and utilizing the violet light of transmutation, where we irradiate the substance with violet light, transmitting it through our hand chakras, or through the use of the digestive grid that we offered in *The Food of Gods* book.

Q: What about being both food and fluid free? How difficult is that?

A: This is an interesting discussion and one I have been focused on this past year. I know that if a person has the right calibration level and have implemented the alternate feeding mechanisms that they can exist without fluid as the cosmic particle flow will hydrate and nourish them. The discussion then is choice and only a handful of people choose this lifestyle today as it is incredibly socially alienating in the western world. Hence most prefer to still drink. Nothing is difficult if we have the right calibration to attract enough cosmic particles.

Q: Are the internal feeding mechanisms really necessary? Can't it be even simpler?

A: If someone is merged in the field of love and has the right calibration level, all they need is the desire to do this. However as a field scientist I prefer to rely on models that everyone can apply to experience all the benefits of The Prana Program. Nonetheless as the field changes, the models do become simpler.

Q: What is a true breatharian?
A: A true breatharian is someone who survives purely from cosmic particles and magnetizing enough of the pranic flow to feed them and maintain health and perfect hydration levels. They neither eat nor drink as they have moved their consciousness beyond the need or desire for food, fluid or flavor.

Q: How many true breatharians have you met?
A: One. Zinaida Baranova in Russia who as at 2005 has been 5 years without food or fluid. She says her biological age is now 30, although she is nearly 70, and tests that we did together in Russia in 2005 proved us both to be extremely healthy. I have met others who have gone without food and fluid for specific periods of time yet when I met them they were choosing to drink for social reasons. I am sure that there are others but many prefer to remain private with this choice and work behind the scenes and I only meet the ones that I need to connect with.

Q: But aren't there thousands now who drink but don't eat as they supplement their liquid only diet with prana?
A: Yes.

Q: How does the true breatharian get their hydration requirements so that they don't experience kidney failure?
A: There are a few methods I have researched for this and we share these in detail in the manual *The Law of Love*. The simplest method that I use personally is the one we will describe in the last part of this book. As many people in Third World countries have limited access to both food and water, we have designed a simple nutrition and hydration program to address this there. Again if the kidneys are being flushed with a strong enough flow of cosmic particles from the universal ocean and if the individual is expecting the kidneys to be hydrated by this flow then their bodies will create and mirror this reality.

Q: Does Zinaida Baranova live the lifestyle, and use the internal feeding mechanisms, that you share?

A: No. She has tapped into this energy purely by the power of devotion and her love for the Christ. She came into this reality in a different way.

Q: Do pranic nourishers all meditate?

A: In order to tune oneself to different reality fields, meditation is one of the most effective tools. It also allows us to access the limitless nature of the pure energy spark within. Through meditation and mind mastery, many pranic nourishers have embedded their conscious awareness in the eternal now and choose to continue with regular meditation just for the joy it. Personally the love flow I feel in meditation is like an incredible meal that satisfies me on all levels and keeps me anchored in the fields of my choice.

Q: Have you ever met anyone who has safely and successfully converted to prana only nourishment without any preparation?

A: Yes, two, but when they were checked their calibration was aligned. Both had vast yogic training in previous timelines although neither had meditated, been on a refined diet or been fit and healthy prior to conversion in this life. The desire to do these things came to them very naturally post conversion.

Q: Post conversion process, which is better?

> *a) To act as a channel to allow the Divine Love and Divine Wisdom Nutrition to flow through us and radiate out into the world thereby transforming both our bio-system and the world simultaneously or*
>
> *b) To build up a reserve of this type of Nutritional force and operate from that cache or well?*

A: Ideally both. Building up energy reserves happens when we apply the lifestyle first as a tune-in program and then utilize it as a daily maintenance program. I have done both and find the combination more powerful than doing just one or the other. Sooner or later we may find we may need to radiate extra which may drain the well, consequently we need to be plugged into a never-ending limitless Source and we also need to keep the radiation pure which the 8 point lifestyle does. Because of the type of food that meditation offers, we find ourselves naturally hungry to be in that silent, loving space anyway especially when we are living in chaotic cities where we can feel as if we are drowning in a denser beat. Existing purely in the Beta field creates emotional, mental and spiritual anorexia and leads humanity into disharmony, war and chaos.

Q: Are meditation practices a key to unlock our ability to transform subtle prana into gross sustenance?

A: Yes definitely – daily meditation PLUS a long term vegan then raw food diet, a well detoxed AND healthy and fit body, a good mind/body connection, a belief that you create your own reality and an understanding of universal law are all beneficial. Studies are now showing how just doing deep, fine and connected breathing regularly is amazingly transformational.

Q: What about the time of instant physical transformation? How come when people use a command or chant nothing seems to instantly change?

A: There are a number of internal and external factors that inhibit this. Firstly there is the strength of the morphogenetic field and what the dominant beat is. This is like a small boy with a soprano voice singing in a choir of 100 men who are baritones, unless his voice carries and is extremely powerful, his sound field will be drowned out. Similarly light eaters are required to tune into the Theta field for our nourishment and live a lifestyle that keeps us tuned to this channel enough to maintain health. Yet if you have only .01% of 1% of the people of this planet doing this, then maintaining this frequency can be difficult due to the beat of the balance of the field. However, thankfully the Theta field radiation is like an atomic blast in power compared to the Beta field radiation, which is like a candle in voltage comparison, so numbers are not the overriding factor here as the Beta field can be transformed by purity and potency.

The next factor is to do with how trusting an individual is of the God within – our DOW – and also how real is the idea that we are a God in form who has all the creative power, healing power and transformational power that we need at our disposal. Many people believe this intellectually but not on a cellular level. Tapping into DOW Power and then witnessing Its flow, and the benefits It brings, all helps to build this trust. In this field, experience is everything, for the flow of Divine Love is not an intellectual affair, and only when we feel this flow within can we trust It enough to surrender and explore Its other attributes.

The third factor is to do with karmic learning and the fourth factor is to do with our Divine blueprint and the role we have agreed to play. Nonetheless, all unfolds perfectly as it should and all we are being asked to do is hold the vision of ourselves as Gods in form, and to act impeccably as if we truly are masters, so that the universe can support us back into the field of Oneness where all possibilities are real and where the highest realities that benefit all are supported into being. The more we do this, the sooner our abilities for instant manifestation become evident individually and en mass.

THE PRANA PROGRAM
Enjoyable & Effective Evolution with Jasmuheen
e-book at http://www.selfempowermentacademy.com.au/htm/cia-education.asp#pranaprogram

---

Brief Conversion Summary

☺ Detoxify yourself physically, emotionally, mentally and spiritually.
☺ Test your calibration levels and ask the below questions.
☺ Refine your calibration via your day to day lifestyle.
☺ Ask the U.F.I. to support your conversion with joy, ease and Grace.

Preparation for Conversion – Self Testing Questions
Use the sway tool and/or tummy breath test tool as outlined earlier to ascertain your answers to the below.

What is your current biological age? _____
(This is a way of checking if your current lifestyle is working for you or against you)
Currently, what percentage of your nourishment comes from prana?   _____%
Currently, what percentage of cosmic particles are hydrating you?   _____%
What is the weight that your body will support you at if you stop eating now?   _____kgs
What is the weight that your body will support you at if you stop drinking now? _____kgs
How long for pranic energies for feeding/hydration to stabilize?   _____
How long until weight stabilizes?   _____
How long until full prana power   - feeding?   _____
                                    - Hydration? _____
What is your current calibration?   _____
What is your ideal biological age?   _____
What do you need to do to support the manifestation of the benefits of The Prana Program?

Increase meditation time?	Yes / No
Change your mental attitudes?	Yes / No
Change belief systems?	Yes / No
Lighten up your diet?	Yes / No
Eat less; if yes, then ask	Yes / No
3>2 meals per day	Yes / No
2>1 meals per day	Yes / No

Other intuitive questions? Ask and test.
Is your body now ready to:-

Go vegetarian?	Yes / No
Go vegan and be dairy free?	Yes / No

THE PRANA PROGRAM
Enjoyable & Effective Evolution with Jasmuheen
e-book at http://www.selfempowermentacademy.com.au/htm/cia-education.asp#pranaprogram

Go to raw foods only?	Yes / No
Exist on fluids and prana only?	Yes / No
Be free of external fluid now?	Yes / No

Wherever you are at be prepared to go to the next level of refinement. You can use the above methods to gain answers to any questions that will allow you to fulfill your dreams.

Also make sure you are super relaxed when you do the testing so that only the Chi force of your DOW moves you. Also cross check your answers and make sure the wording of your questions is not ambiguous.

Q: Can you give an exact step by step method to test our personal calibration since this is so important?

A: Yes.

- ☺ Firstly be still and tune into your DOW.
- ☺ When you feel connected and centered via meditation, stand comfortably.
- ☺ Relax your knees and sway from side to side so that your system is loose and can be easily moved by a strong wind for example.
- ☺ Ask your DOW to express itself through you via movement. To sway you forward for a 'yes' answer and backwards for a 'no' answer.
- ☺ Then ask if it is important for you to now know your personal calibration as per David Hawkins's calibration testing system in the book *Power vs Force*.
- ☺ Keep asking as you allow yourself to be moved forward or backward. If you get a 'yes' proceed, if you get a 'no' then stop as it is not relevant at this time.
- ☺ For a 'yes', then state:
- ☺ 'My personal calbration is more than 200 – 'yes' or 'no''.
- ☺ If 'yes' state 'my personal calibration is more than 300'.
- ☺ If 'yes' test again, 'my personal calibration is more than 400'.
- ☺ Be still with each statement and wait for the forward or backward movement to come as you chant each one, do not ask re the next level until you have a response to the last one.
- ☺ Keep testing until you get a 'no' response.
- ☺ Then say for example, 'my personal calibration is more than 450' (if you got a 'no' for more than 500) and determine the exact number.

Q: What if our calibration is in the suggested range, does this automatically guarantee success with our conversion?

A: Unfortunately not necessarily as everything may be perfect but your mindest may not be anchored in the cells as a real trust and knowing and doubt can interfere with pranic flow. Also sometimes it is just not the right time. E.g. for sometime now I have been able to maintain a fluid free existence yet intuitively it still doesn't feel to be the right time for me to do this. When I check my DOW just says 'be patient and trust'. So I am.

⋖ 5 ⋗

Social Scenes

PRANA AND SOCIAL BEHAVIOUR

Q: Many are now living holistically and are accessing the Alpha-Theta-Delta zones due to their lifestyle, and so they find they are becoming increasingly sensitive. This sensitivity often makes them feel as if they must be more reclusive as they do not like mingling in the denser Beta-Alpha fields of community life. There are also often estrangements that occur as an Alpha-Theta field dweller moves out of the 'normal' relatable range of family and friends. Can you comment more on this? What has your research found?

A: A Dimensional Biofield Technician, and spiritual initiate, is someone who has learnt to work with all fields and who – ideally – can exist in harmony in any field without disruption to their own field. As we have already discussed, the two most powerful tools we have to selectively absorb the frequencies we want from the world are:-

a) Our intention, will and attitude, i.e. the absorption versus radiation game, and
b) the use of the Bio-Shield devices which we discuss in Chapter 11 in *The Food of Gods* book.
c) I also feel it is helpful to understand how to influence an existing field and how to weave a new field to support us in a more nurturing manner and again this was discussed in detail in *The Food of Gods*.

It is also beneficial to understand that accessing the channel of Divine Nutrition is not something that happens just to the lucky ones or the blessed or the Holy Ones. Anyone can tap into pranic nourishment. However it is still a daily challenge to be able to exist in a predominantly Beta-Alpha field and still get enough nourishment from the Theta field to maintain health. This is why our energetic hook-ins and Bio-Shield devices are so helpful as they allow us to control the pranic flow. Also the daily practice of Kriya-Yoga and Surya-Yoga and techniques like the 'Love Breath' meditation are most helpful in moving us into more supportive fields as like attracts like.

Another problem mentioned is the fact that as we consciously shift our frequencies to anchor ourselves in more nourishing fields, we do move out of relatable range with those who choose not to frequency match us. This is particularly noticeable among family and friends who may not understand our choice of a more refined diet or sensitive lifestyle.

In response to this I would like to share that we have our bloodline family and also our global family and the ideal way of sharing is with unconditional love. So to make sure you give and get this type of loving, ask your DOW to bring you people with whom you can have a mutually beneficial and supportive relationship. Next when you are with family focus on sharing things that bring mutual pleasure rather than focusing on your differences.

Q: One of the biggest problems people have with a prana only lifestyle is the social readjustment that is required as so many social interactions revolve around food. How do you recommend people deal with this?
A: Part of our learning curve with this journey is learning how to spend time in social situations with food and also creating more social situations away from food e.g. movies, beach/nature walks, board/card games. Personally I try to arrange my social interaction with relatives around activities other than the sharing of food.

Q: When many people hear about your choice to abstain from eating the typical response is: "Why would you want to do that? Eating is such an enjoyable experience." How do you respond to this?
Q: I agree and the biggest problem many of 'the prana eaters' have, is dealing with a lack of variety of flavor and let's face it – eating food can bring amazing pleasure to the mouth and stomach and bonding over meals can be fun. Still there are many ways to gain pleasure in life and most people become involved in this for the freedom it offers. It's great to be really free to be able to choose, to not 'have to' eat but still be strong and healthy.

So if we feel like eating for the sheer pleasure of it now and then, we do, but we don't *need* to eat and the benefits of this are really quite amazing. There are actually more benefits to a diet of 'light' than a physical food diet. No illness, more energy, no weight problems, extra money, extra time, no fear of 'what will I do if there was no access to food' like with the 2004 Tsunami and the 2005 Hurricane problems. A prana diet, a fruitarian or raw food diet, also appears to slow down the aging process. It is early days with our research but we know that in time the benefits will be proven to be so.

Q: With people constantly saying that physical food is a gift from God and that to not eat is 'unnatural' and is to deny yourself a great pleasure; how do you handle this?

A: As I have already stated, there are many ways to nourish ourselves apart from the usual choices of food, or indiscriminate sex, or drugs that dull or over-stimulate our mind like television for example. I am not saying that any of these things are 'bad' per se, just that we have not yet been well educated as to alternative forms of nourishment, particularly true emotional nourishment.

The sharing of food with friends and in social settings does bring great pleasure, not just to the palette but also on emotional bonding levels. This is one of the reasons that some light eaters still eat from time to time even though their bio-systems have been freed from the need for physical food. For me personally, one the best 'meals' I can give myself is listening to sacred music or a walk along a beach where I can simultaneously bathe in – and absorb – sun and wind and water prana. Another 'meal' for me is a walk in a rainforest or to meditate on a mountain in the dusk or dawn light.

Q: Do you have any statistics on the people who do this?

A: Our 1998 research found that our oldest Light Ambassador was a 93-year-old woman in Austria and the average age is 52. Also 55% are women and while many have been long term meditators of between 5 to 20 plus years, 87% were experienced with metaphysics. The majority were also long term vegetarians, vegans or raw foodists and 60% were committed to a life of selfless humanitarian service. Most do this to experience more of the love and power of their DOW, flooding our system with Its love to the degree It then feeds us is an interesting journey.

Q: What type of people become pranic nourishers and how do they deal with public reaction?

A: Many are well researched and have studied metaphysics intuitively, then consciously, for many lifetimes. While we now remember and trust this knowing, we are also realistic to know that our thought processes can trigger feelings of discomfort within the mass consciousness as our lifestyle challenges the beliefs of the status quo. There are also areas of discussion that only those who have begun the activation the the 4/5th's of the brain needed to comprehend our ideals and visions can appreciate, hence we recognize the need for, and promote, holistic education. By bringing this information to the public, we hope to plant seeds of hope and love and joy in the hearts of all who feel this is a reality of worthwhile co-creation due to all its benefits and not just the physical nourishment aspect.

Q: What is their common agenda?

A: Most realize that The Prana Program is not just about eating or not eating. In the economically developed and industrialized cultures it is about being free to be in our power and choose without fear. For the cultures and countries experiencing starvation it is about freedom from the need to die from lack of physical nourishment. We are offering the invitation for humanity to choose to collectively create a model of reality that manifests positive personal and planetary transformation in a way that honors all lifeforms. How long this will take will be dependant on how many hearts and minds hear, relate and act upon this message and all research.

Q: What do you feel is the main challenge for someone demonstrating a prana only nourishment?

A: While we are learning together, sharing together, then demonstrating together, many of my fellow travelers find that the main disadvantage is extreme social alienation that occurs from this choice as the majority of western culture eats for the pleasure of emotional-based reasons and so much of social interaction is focused on eating. There is also a slight problem with lack of flavor for those who choose not to indulge in the odd mouthful of flavor for pleasure. As mentioned before, many pranic nourishers choose to have the odd taste to satisfy the taste buds while others say that they have moved beyond the consciousness of food.

Q: You often tell people not to claim that they never eat even if they never do. Why? Surely this is an interesting claim to make especially if it is true?

A: Claims like this create too many restrictions in our current state of global consciousness. What if a pranic nourisher needs to go into a shop to buy food for a friend or family member who is due to visit them and someone sees them, takes a photo and says, "See I told you he/she must be eating, I saw him/her in a shop buying food!"

Also to never say never eliminates the inner child's reaction to such restrictions. I treat pranic feeding like an alcoholic with an addiction, I just take one day at a time especially in the earlier years when we unhook our emotional/social addictions to food.

Thirdly, things change over time. Once you have proven this ability to yourself by living it long enough to do so, some people then structure new social habits that are a little less restrictive such as sharing one meal a week, or a meal once a month, for social reasons. As I keep stressing, this is not a path of restriction, or allowing ourselves to be limited by others perceived ideas about us, it is a path of freedom.

THE PRANA PROGRAM
Enjoyable & Effective Evolution with Jasmuheen
e-book at http://www.selfempowermentacademy.com.au/htm/cia-education.asp#pranaprogram

PRANA AND PARENTING

Before we begin the Q & A's on this, I would like to share that we are now experiencing an influx of some very aware children e.g. the Indigo's and the Crystals in particular. Please do further research on these so that you can understand some of their proclivities particularly their lack of interest in physical food. Doreen Virtue has written a lovely little book on *The Crystal Children* many of whom are natural light eaters.

Q: How does a "prana only nourishment regime" affect motherhood? Can a pranic nourisher lactate?

A: I have only personally known one woman who has given birth while a practicing pranic nourisher although I have heard of many others. They all had no problems lactating and the children were born completely healthy. This goes back to the understanding that a change in mind set is required where we fully comprehend that when nourishment comes from the universal life force, the human physical body remains vital and healthy.

Q: Can two people who are on prana only nourishment still conceive and have a child?

A: Yes and yes.

Q: Can one be a pranic nourisher from birth or it there a minimum age?

A: Many children incarnating in the world today have no desire to eat and prefer a more liquid diet. This is a natural consequence of their higher vibration and conscious awareness of all that they are. Regarding a minimum age, this would be dependent on how supportive the family and social environment is, as many children are easily influenced, away from their natural intuitive abilities, by less aware adults who the children may be led to believe know more due to their adult status. (A highly disputable idea in esoteric thought as old, wise souls often dwell in very small forms.)

Q: Does a pure prana diet affect growth/development/body size?

A: Remember all growth occurs perfectly IF we are being well nourished and prana is the purest form of nourishment that we have. Also many people practicing this successfully are tuned instruments either developing, or already possessing, great command over their molecular structure and can manipulate body size and shape at will through re-programming and lifestyle choice. The body is a bio-computer, the mind is the software package, life is the print-out of the two. If one does not like life or any aspect of it, we can rewrite the software program and alter how the universe responds to us. Quality thinking brings quality life, limitless thinking brings limitless life. Provided the prana flow is strong enough to provide all a person needs then there is no problem with growth and development.

Q: What do you advise women who want to convert to a pure prana diet but who also wish to have children soon?

A: I recommend two choices:-

    a) Convert to the prana only nourishment stream and make sure you are 100% convinced it is working for you BEFORE you have children as any doubts can inhibit flow and could possibly affect a healthy pregnancy.

    b) Have children first and then slowly convert when it feels right later.

Also confirm your calibration levels to see whether you are in the correct range to do this as this will help your confidence. If it is too low you would obviously not proceed.

Q: How do you recommend the parent of a child, who rarely likes to eat, deal with this?

A: With love and understanding and by being well informed of the reality we discuss in this manual. Education eliminates fear which comes from ignorance. A parent needs to act responsibly and it is easy to tell if a child is a natural pranic nourisher as regardless of what they eat – type and quantity of food – they will exhibit all the signs of glowing health. Children who suffered from lack of nourishment are often lethargic, may have problems with concentration and mental clarity, can be aggressive and are often ill. You can also check their calibration.

Q: What if a child mainly wants to drink?

A: You can either:-

    a) trust their choice with this and remind them that prana must be delivering all their vitamins or

    b) make sure that they have all their nutritional needs fulfilled in a fluid form they enjoy.

I also recommend that these children be educated to understand the power prana has to nourish them and again to also check the child's calibration to see if it is of the magnitude to attract a good mix of cosmic particles for nourishment.

Q: Can you tell us more about the Lotus, Indigo and Crystal Children?

A: Throughout this century, different models of humanity have been born and each model has had a specific purpose. The LOTUS children are the wave of the baby boomers who came with a huge desire for inner and outer peace, which they recognized could only come through self knowledge, and so they embraced free love and/or eastern mysticism with its yoga and meditation principles and later self-help therapy. Their mission was to be the miracle seekers and to lay the foundation for a new millennium of a peaceful, sensitive co-existence and to be a radiant example of masters who can harmoniously and happily exist in a world of illusion. The LOTUS children come to bridge the worlds.

When the baby boomers grew older, perhaps tired and more complacent, the INDIGO children came to shake up our systems further and say "Hey, things could run a little better here for the whole. My standards are higher than this and my needs aren't being met." Highly creative and sensitive they are demanding to be listened to and ask for a refinement of our educational and social systems for they come as the bringers of change. Misunderstood, the Indigos often end up ignored, seen as 'too difficult' or sedated; yet they too are just the seekers of miracles.

Next came the Miracle Makers, the CRYSTAL children. The crystal children are children awake to their DOW nature and they have incarnated to bring many gifts. Often free of karmic imbalances, they come to inspire, to heal, to bridge the animal and human worlds by honoring and loving all life and the environment of Earth. Choosing light (often prana based) diets, many are telepathic, all are empathetic and many are examples of the power of unconditional love. Their role is to smooth the way after the baby boomers and Indigos have shaken up the systems and reset standards to focus again on more joy. The Crystal children come to be inspirational examples of love in action and they need little from us except our love and appreciation. Working together with the Lotus Children, the Indigos and now the Crystals are redefining what true pleasure means for they know that pleasure comes from creating a more harmonious world.

PRANA AND OTHER FAMILY MEMBERS – HARMONIZING HOUSEHOLDS

Q: When a person begins to live on a prana only nourishment stream, what is the best way to deal with friends and family?
A: It is important to understand that we all have different blueprints and pre-encodements to fulfill and to respect that. Family will choose this path IF and WHEN it feels right for them. The best we can do is to be a healthy and happy example of this lifestyle choice which allows people to be aware of the freedom of this possibility. Over the last decade pranic feeders have noticed a very interesting social phenomenon, which is that many people who spend time in our fields automatically begin to

eat less and feel much better for it. As the energy that radiates through us is love and as our personal biofield has been imprinted with the knowing, based on experience, that we do not need to take nourishment from physical food, this tends to imprint the fields of people around us.

Q: How?

A: By feeding them via our presence which allows them quicker access to the Theta-Delta field within their cells which then provides certain benefits – like intuitive knowledge, increased sensitivity as in clairsentience and the desire to eat less etc. The highest alchemical action that we can attain is the transformation of our bio-system into a DOW Power radiation station, an act that provides us naturally with the by-products of pranic nourishment and this becomes evident to people when they spend time with you and witness the Grace in your life.

Q: How do your daughters, parents and husband feel about your path?

A: Great – I'm blessed that they love and accept me – although I'm sure that at times they have seen me to be like a mad professor. As I have been pursuing my metaphysical interests virtually my whole life, everyone is used to my experiments in human potential and understand my blueprints and drive. This of course all comes about due to constant clear communication. Also when family see that you are healthy and happy with your choices they are generally more supportive. My parents have since crossed over but while they were alive, I kept them well informed as to all my relevant research. Good communication and education are the key.

Q: Are they interested in pursuing it themselves?

A: My youngest daughter is now 28 and has never had meat and my oldest daughter is a lacto-ovo vegetarian, both love yoga and are aware of the power of positive thinking and work with the universal field. All my family are spiritually active in their way and are aware of the higher possibilities in life. My husband has been a vegan, exerciser and weight lifter, and has also meditated, for decades. My grandparents were psychic and lived their lives convinced they were guided by higher powers so in my family I am hardly leading the way into unchartered waters although I am probably a little more extreme than most. I trust that my family will choose what is perfect for them and I love them all as unconditionally as I am able.

Q: How did you deal with the concern of your parents and family when you began to live only on pranic nourishment?

A: Education. I provided them with simple research, did the necessary medical tests to prove I was healthier than ever and initially I set out to be a shining example of someone healthy and happy and obviously enjoying my lifestyle in a beneficial way so there was nothing for them to worry about.

Q: Have you ever pretended to still eat to make a social situation more comfortable for a family member?

A: Yes sometimes this is beneficial for them. It is not always appropriate to draw attention to ourselves in social settings by our choice not to eat in the usual way. Some social situations may be set up to focus on someone else in your family and they do not want the focus to go to their non-eating spouse or parent, so attending these events, taking a small plate of food and pushing it around the plate without eating can help circumvent too much curiosity and keep the focus where it belongs. This was an action plan my youngest daughter once formulated that worked well for the situation that we were in.

Q: What if you are the cook of the family and no longer choose to eat? Isn't this constant exposure to food a little challenging?

A: It can be for some. I taught my children to cook when they were very young and we shared this task and having your family each take turns in meal preparation helps to alleviate this challenge. Some pranic nourishers delegate this to husbands and children and provide healthy take out for them on the nights it is their turn to provide a meal for the family. Good communication and restructuring of these responsibilities can help to alleviate this issue also. Again all of this depends on the level of respect and good clear communication in a family plus the mutual desire to create win/win situations for all. Where family are less flexible it can be more of an issue.

PRANA AND EATING DISORDERS

Q: What guidance do you have for anorexics or bulimics?

A: Focus on getting fit and healthy – physically, emotionally, mentally and spiritually. Life's too short for sorrow and there truly is a lot of fun to be had. Learn to meditate and how to form positive and empowering relationships – first with yourself and then with your family and friends. Anorexia generally is a result of lack of self love whereas living on prana is the opposite as it requires great self love and awareness of who we really are.

Q: Did you ever suffer from an eating disorder?

A: No, I never had time to develop one. I was always too busy exploring and enjoying the possibilities in life. I also had the luxury of a very loving and stimulating childhood plus an early interest in self mastery on an experiential level.

PRANA, SEXUALITY AND OUR ROMANTIC RELATIONSHIPS

Q: Many people living on prana only also say that their sexual energy changes, can you elaborate on this further?
A: For many pranic nourishers in partnership, the common practice is tantra or the Taoist sexual energy flow which stimulate brain orgasms, heart orgasms and full body orgasms. The conscious practice of this incorporates the sexual energy (lower base and sacral chakras) with the spiritual energy (crown and brow chakras) and the unconditional love energy (heart chakra) via the Microcosmic Orbit technique (as outlined in Mantak Chia's *Taoist Secrets of Love*).

Others may choose celibacy where celibacy is a choice made not from lack of opportunity for sexual expression but for intentional conscious transmutation of the sexual life force energy into a higher – more refined – creative vibration. A healthy body is a sexual body, hence the sexual energies must be transmuted into a higher vibration or utilized through either procreation or tantric sharing.

Q: Can two people still have a good sexual relationship if only one of them is on The Prana Program and the other chooses to still regularly eat?
A: Obviously for any relationship to be successful, the individuals must resonate together in a beneficial way. Many good relationships exist where couples have very different interests however people choosing The Prana Program are often very sensitive to energies so provided your partner's overall resonance is supportive and harmonious to you then this is not a problem.

Q: What if this is not the case? What if this lifestyle choice is causing conflict with a partner, how do you suggest it be dealt with then?
A: One thing I often share with people is to have the courage to go beyond tradition and to structure a relationship so that it works for all parties. To do this you need alot of awareness, tenderness, clarity and good communication plus sound self knowledge of what is right for you. For example, at the moment I prefer to live in my own private ashram and maximize my meditation and solitude time, this choice means that I see my husband only six days of every month which suits us both. He lives in his ashram and I in mine and for most of the month we live as celibate yogis.

While this may not suit younger people who are still raising children, it is an option for others. For those in conflict with their different lifestyles who still wish to live together then there are various techniques that can be utilized to create harmony in the home field.

Q: Such as?
A: There are three powerful tools that I use as set programs and codes of intention. These are the "DOW Match" code, the "Perfect Harmony all fields now!" code plus the "Perfect Resolution" tool. Although simple tools, they work beautifully for people who are aware of the power of programming and that thoughts create reality.

Q: Can you explain these in more detail so that others in conflict can apply them and gain benefit?
A: a) "DOW match!"
We say this telepathically while sending a beam of heart love to the person we wish to connect to in this way. It moves our communication beyond mind, ego and past life influences and allows us to communicate DOW to DOW in a way that is beneficial to all.

b) "Perfect Harmony all fields now!"
Again said telepathically with the intention to exist in perfect harmony with all fields, this provides a clear command to the U.F.I. to support you in this specific way.

c) "Perfect Resolution Now! Win/win/win!"
When said telepathically with conviction and an intention to resolve a situation and for the U.F.I. to deliver a solution that creates a win for you, a win for others and a win for the world, this command opens us to other levels of universal support, solutions and insight. It always works provided we do the above and remember we are made in the image of the Divine and as masters the U.F.I. will serve us if our hearts are pure.

SOCIAL SCENES SUMMARY

- ☺ Holistic education will create a more supportive field of The Prana Program so be patient.
- ☺ Be honest with self and others but also learn to be circumspect regarding The Prana Program and act appropriately.

- ☺ Create a win/win/win situation regarding this choice and regarding family and friends and maintain good clear communication.
- ☺ Create more social sharing scenes independent of food.
- ☺ Be an impeccable example of self mastery but do it harmoniously with all.

☙ 6 ❧

Global Issues ~ Gifts & Growth

PAST, PRESENT & FUTURE

Q: What is the past status of The Prana Program?
A: For thousands of years, prana has been utilized by the yogis in the east to nourish them on many levels, including as food for the physical system. Many civilizations have successfully used micro food, or prana direct from solar nourishment, to keep them healthy including the Mayans, Native American Indians and the Egyptians to name a few. Confined to the secret teachings of Indigenous and eastern cultures, in the past western cultures have been largely uneducated, and thus unaware, as to its gifts.

Q: What is the current status of The Prana Program?
A: Due to our extensive media work, The Prana Program and its gift of nourishment has now been anchored in the morphogenetic field with over 10% of the western population being aware of it on some level.

PRANA FEEDING PROGRAM
1. GRASS ROOTS SPREAD IN WESTERN WORLD
2. THIRD WORLD COUNTRIES PROGRAM

PRANA – PEACE NETWORKS
ALL THOSE COMMITTED TO GLOBAL UNITY AND HARMONY WHO ACCESS PRANA POWER AS DIVINE LOVE IN THEIR MEDITATIONS

PRANA – HEALTH MAINTENANCE NETWORKS
TAI CHI, QIGONG, MARTIAL ARTS AND YOGA NETWORKS

PRANA AND HEALING NETWORKS
REIKI NETWORKS
PRANIC HEALING NETWORKS
QIGONG NETWORKS

Q: What do you predict as its future status?

A: If we can gain access to educational and media channels in a more positive and less sensationalistic way and if we continue with the personal experiential growth, then I forsee that this reality and all of the benefits of The Prana Program will become firmly established as a natural nourishment option for humanity within a very short time. I would like to see at least as many books on this subject in western bookstores and libraries as there are on vegetarianism, meditation and alternative healing.

Q: Are there any famous pranic nourishers?

A: The Comte St Germain, who some say penned Shakespeare's plays, was never seen to eat or drink in public and maintained a non-aging physical form for centuries. Other Himalayan yogis may take food offered in love from their devotees, yet do not require sustenance via food. Many other Spiritual Masters have commonly undergone 40 day retreats with neither food nor water. More recently Prahlad Jani, Hira Ratan Manek, Zinaida Baranova and myself have come under public scrutiny for our experiential work in this field. Currently a fifteen year old boy in India – Ram Bahadur Bantan – is now gathering attention re his personal experience of this.

Q: Your first book on the prana program was called Pranic Nourishment – Nutrition for the New Millenium (also called Living on Light). Why do you consider prana to be nutrition for the new millenium?

A: It has been wonderful nutrition for all millenniums but due to the internet and our global communications networks we can now share of the benefits of The Prana Program more easily. After a decade of experiential research we have since discovered the additional benefits of increasing the pranic flow, that when embraced will create a more effective and enjoyable evolutionary path for all, as we have since discovered that it can eliminate hunger on all levels.

Q: You have spoken of the personal benefits earlier but what are some of the global benefits of increasing the pranic flow through the body?

A: Apart from increasing our individual health and happiness levels the global economic and environmental impact of this is astounding. For example, every few minutes we lose acres of Amazon rainforest so that crops can be grown to feed cattle which are then slaughtered to feed people. The adoption of a pure prana or even a vegetarian diet eliminates this immediately thus supporting the evolution of a more compassionate and kind human species. Mahatma Gandhi once said that you can tell a lot about a nation by the way it treats its animals.

Some other global benefits are:-

a) Minimization of the need for and use of insecticides and pesticides as we decrease our need for crop production, by increasing our dependence on more natural internal feeding systems for prana instead, thus reducing environmental pollution.

b) Minimization of garbage disposal from food production, distribution and consumption, as we decrease our consumption need by increasing the pranic flow.

c) Decrease in our dependence on pharmaceuticals as we increase our health and longevity levels so we can redirect financial resources into other research fields.

d) Decrease our dependence on medical support systems such as medical care, hospitals, and tax dollars spent on illness support systems etcetera as we increase health and longevity by increasing the prana flow. These dollars can be redirected to aid, education and housing the less fortunate in all countries.

e) Increasing the pranic flow increases feelings of compassion, love, kindness and Oneness thus decreasing our dependence on psychiatric care, and eliminating social feelings of isolation and loneliness that are increasing in western cultures and thus also decreasing the growing suicide rate.

f) Decrease in the growing obesity problems and the current increase in spending to address this. As we increase pranic flow we are fed on *all* levels and therefore eliminate physical, emotional, mental and spiritual hunger. Most people eat for emotional reasons. Both anorexia and obesity is generally a sign of a lack of holistic education and are also often from a lack of self love.

g) Increasing the pranic flow within a person also brings them into an improved state of inner balance and harmony so that we can utilize the world's resources in a more effective and humane manner.

h) Helps with the redistribution of resources as the 'haves' use less so that there is more for the 'have nots' – provided we distribute resources more compassionately. Nonetheless increasing the pranic flow naturally increases our compassion levels as we glimpse more of the bigger picture in life as increasing the pranic flow also expands our consciousness.

i) Changes our personal field radiation so that our presence feeds rather than drains the world.

Q: *How many pranic nourishers are their globally and where are they found?*
A: As I travel I hear the stories of many journeys with this process and as at end 2004 we guesstimate approximately 20,000 people were existing purely on prana with approximately sixty four thousand now able to but with many of these not choosing to. (*U.F.I. statistics*) As we generally work

only with the innernet, and do not seek to extensively document this, we are not aware of names and places world-wide and no-one has consciously tracked how far it has spread. There has been no need to do this as we understood at the beginning of our work that this is a natural path of human evolution and will come into being and acceptance in its own time, although we can speed this up via holistic education programs that also include The Prana Program findings.

While it may seem to be unusual in the west, we have been long aware of how it is common practice for the immortalists and yogis in India and the Himalayas to go without food and sleep and even fluid for substantial periods of time and how many can also change their body temperature at will or shapeshift. This is also a common occurrence among the Qigong community, and for many other people who are working consciously with and transmitting higher frequencies, but we are unable to estimate the numbers in these communities.

Note: Our desire to speed this up is not motivated by a wish to see a non-eating world but by a humane desire to eliminate health and hunger challenges which are simply unnecessary.

Q: *What about negativity and all the conflict happening around the world?*

A: It's just one movie of reality, and we've really come a long way. There are still global hotspots that need some attention and many of us in our service have recognized the need to refine things, because while a lot of systems do work, not all of them work for the good of all. The Universal Law of Resonance says that what we focus on becomes our reality; like attracts like, so when we understand that every thought is sent out and attracts like energy which strengthens it, then comes back to us like a boomerang, then we become very aware of what thoughts, words and actions we want to indulge in. Many have had enough of killing, chaos and confusion. I know from my own experience that we can change our field of reality to another more harmonious and honoring channel. It's just mind power, I've seen people live in heaven here on Earth, others in hell. And most of it is just a reflection of our own perception. "Receive it how you perceive it" is a common metaphysical saying.

I think that the message coming through so many now, is that we have the power to retune this world so that all have the happiness they desire, but it must start with ourselves, as individuals make up the masses.

Q: *You talk of the implications for world hunger. How practical is the idea of taking The Prana Program into famine areas?*

A: For many years I have felt that we need to redistribute resources more effectively on this planet, and that you don't give the starving spirituality, you give them food. Billions of people live in poverty including urban dwellers and millions in developing countries who live in life threatening conditions.

THE PRANA PROGRAM
Enjoyable & Effective Evolution with Jasmuheen
e-book at http://www.selfempowermentacademy.com.au/htm/cia-education.asp#pranaprogram

While one billion live on less than $1 USD per day and another two billion live on approximately $2 USD per day, research on alternate nutritional sources must be supported. Prior to the global war on terrorism, $868 billion was spent annually on armaments and yet warfare is the biggest human cause of famine and at the time of writing this it was reported that the U.S.A. is spending over 4 billion dollars a week on the war in Iraq. Hence many supporting The Prana Program feel that our priorities need to change so that these challenges can be addressed more humanely and some of the causative factors behind terrorism eliminated.

Q: You often talk of the power of prayer and programming in The Prana Program. How can this aid starving children for example?

A: While we will address the 'starving children' issue shortly, people often underestimate the power of the human heart and mind and the benefits of mental programming and the power of set intention and prayer. In 1997 I heard the story of an orphanage in Germany who after the war had very little food. While one group of children were starving, another group remained really happy and healthy. The young children in the healthy group had a carer, and they asked her what she was doing different. She said they just started the day by forming a circle and praying to Mary and Jesus to love them and care for them, and make sure they got through the experience without harm. Because these kids believed in these prayers, they stayed healthy and were fine. If guided by an aware adult, our children can exist in very supportive paradigms of which The Prana Program is a part.

Q: Can you describe your education work with the Light Ambassadry and the M.A.P.S. Ambassadry?

A: The M.A.P.S. Ambassadry is the Movement of an Awakened Positive Society. It's an umbrella organization with no physical structure; a consciousness movement of people dedicated to positive planetary and personal progression. There are people all over the world involved in this, from the health professions to metaphysical workers, spiritualist churches, political and green activists – these are all people who loosely fall under that umbrella.

Living on prana is part of the Light Ambassadry work and we have a particular agenda, which we call the World Health/World Hunger project, meaning hunger for love, health, happiness as well as actual hunger. We're focused on emptying the hospitals, redirecting resources away from pharmaceuticals and towards preventative medicine. The extreme of that is, if you are very disciplined and dedicated in your lifestyle, you can bring yourself to a level of fitness where you no longer need to take nourishment from food and you never get sick. It's interesting to note the IMS research that says how we spent $179 billion on pharmaceuticals in 1998 and World Bank recent research stated that we only need $350 billion per annum to eliminate global poverty which is less than 1/3 of our current annual military budget.

Q: Do you really believe that The Prana Program will eventually be socially acceptable?

A: Definitely as the fact is that good holistic education is a powerful tool. On an evolutionary level, it is interesting to note how socially unacceptable it is now in Australia and the U.S.A for people to still smoke cigarettes. Due to massive re-education programs and bans on smoking in public places, cigarette smoking is now seen as socially unacceptable due to its associated health hazards and passive smoking statistics. In future I can see the same attitudes evolving around meat eating whereby it will become socially unacceptable to be involved with the slaughter of animal life – directly or indirectly. As people are re-educated into acting with more kindness and compassion on all levels, global vegetarianism will become a preferred and obvious option. Once there, then The Prana Program's light nourishment aspect will also be more acceptable for those wishing to go to an even more refined dietary level and their contribution to resource sustainability will be appreciated and noted as their health and life quality levels change.

PRANA AND HEALTH

Q: You say that The Prana Program can eliminate all dis-ease individually and globally. How?

A: Because it can nourish a person on all levels. Physical disease usually results from lack of emotional, mental and spiritual nourishment as well as toxic eating habits and lack of exercise. Humanity has entered into a stage of evolution where we need to reassess what we term true nourishment, as for the first time in our history we have the extreme of approximately 1.2 billion people suffering malnutrition from lack of physical nourishment and 1.2 billion people suffering from obesity related problems due to incorrect physical nourishment and addictions to fast foods served to placate a fast society. For many people eating and the 'pleasure' food brings is an emotional addiction in an attempt to satisfy a deeper hunger. At this time in our evolution we are being intuitively guided to encourage pleasures that promote and sustain physical, emotional, mental and spiritual fitness in all.

Q: Do all people on a prana only program never get sick anymore?

A: This depends on three things:-

a) Their personal calibration levels;
b) how active they are in the world and how much they allow this activity to expand them beyond their limits and how good they are at self nurturing and also
c) their service agenda. Sometimes it may be in someone's service agenda to manifest a disease and then cure it and share how they cured it with the world. Pioneers are in all fields.

Q: Can you explain this further?

A: Generally if a person maintains their calibration levels at more than 630* they will be out of the field of disease creation unless they are overextending themselves and/or not nurturing themselves enough. For example, for many years I worked 120 hours per week when I was at home and traveled for eight months of each year living in highly polluted environments. For most of this time I rarely experienced even a cold and maintained great health and energy levels due to the nature of my service work which kept me tuned. One of the benefits of The Prana Program is that our capacity to multi-task and work long hours can expand dramatically if required.

*This level of 630 will change as the morphogenetic field changes.

Q: The Prana Program must generate immense healing energy; how does it manifest?

A: It depends on each individual's blueprint. If your assignment here is to help people never to get sick, then those abilities are magnified through this process. Many people in healing roles have found they get increased levels of sensitivity and increased clairaudience and clairvoyance which are by-products of living on pure prana. Quite a lot of people in the healing profession have chosen to live in a prana only nourishment stream, because of the different gifts that they gain from this, particularly regarding the potency of the energy they can access and channel in the healing process.

Q: How have you directed the energy that you personally have gained to healing?

A: To me personal reality is just a movie and we are the script writers, stars and directors and we can serve here and make a positive difference with our lives or not. In my movie, one of my roles is about inspiring self responsibility for self healing, and also living life to our highest potential, so my energy is directed to healing through re-education and providing lifestyle tools for preventative medicine. What I have discovered with my own harmonious healing journey is that just as there are certain steps that occur to create a disease, we can also uncreate that same disease – i.e. heal it – via taking steps that the body recommends. The tools to gain this unique information from a person's body I am now also able to share as self healing is empowering and unhooks us from medical and pharmaceutical dependency.

Q: What about scientific research regarding prana emissions and healing?
Answer with Eltrayan: In the scientific investigations conducted by the Chinese it is noted that the external prana emitted by a 'healing' practitioner, carries different information from the prana of a non-practitioner. It is well known that all body parts, internal organs and tissues of the human body have a weak magnetic field. However, when a pranic practitioner enters into a state of pranic emission, the magnetic intensity of certain places of the body surface can be ten thousand to one million times stronger than that of internal organs. That is, ten thousand to one million times stronger than a pranic non-practitioner.

Pranic healing was considered for many years to be a kind of psychological treatment, and this point of view is still quite popular in the west. There are some reasons behind it. For instance co-operation, especially psychological co-operation from the patient, is important during treatment. However, scientific experiments have shown that liquid crystal molecules rotate under the influence of external prana, thereby demonstrating that external pranic healing is not just a psychological treatment. It has objective effects independent of any psychological dimension. Numerous cases of pranic healing of an extraordinary nature are reported by Chinese scientific experiments, probably the most dramatic being the healing of bone fractures, with the bones being x-rayed both before and after the pranic treatment, and demonstrating the bones having knitted and healed within hours .

PRANA & RELIGION – Harmonizing the fields enjoyably.

While many religious paths talk about 'attaining higher glories' or ascension, or they talk about gaining 'divine favor'; in the science of the fields both of these can be measured by the flow of Grace which also responds to personal calibration. A joyous flow of synchronicity, Grace comes to those whose thoughts words and actions support the positive evolution of the greater good.

Q: How does The Prana Program work with people's religious beliefs?
A: Generally it tends to add another layer to people's existing beliefs. Over the years I have spoken to and trained people of all walks of life and all religions. Anyone who has had some type of experience of their Divine nature seems to be able to understand this reality when it is fully presented to them and in terms they can relate to. As we know language can unify or separate.

THE PRANA PROGRAM
Enjoyable & Effective Evolution with Jasmuheen
e-book at http://www.selfempowermentacademy.com.au/htm/cia-education.asp#pranaprogram

***

Q: Does a person need to believe in God to successfully be fed by prana?

A: Not necessarily but they need to be open to the power of love and understand the intelligence and power of the universal field and its capability in delivering an alternative way of being nourished. Many have experienced prana's healing powers through Reiki and various energy transference modalities. Many have experienced Its powers of intuitive guidance through their inner voice or "gut instinct" and many have experienced Its love flow in meditation. Having done this, then accepting Its ability to nourish us is not a huge leap. Whether we then term this force God, or not, is really an individual choice. *It* doesn't care what we call It, the universal force of prana is just happy that we acknowledge and experience It at all for It expands the more we identify with It.

Q: What is your personal religion?

A: My personal preference is the experience of the universal field of love and the benefits It brings to us all when we merge with It consciously. So if it needs to be identified then my 'religion' is the action of kindness, compassion, harmony and love.

Q: Can a person maintain their religious beliefs and still apply The Prana Program?

A: Definitely. The Prana Program is just another layer however their success will depend on whether their religious beliefs are based on love, compassion and respect for all life as these things powerfully influence our personal field of resonance and whether we can magnetize enough cosmic particles to keep us healthy. Hate, fear and separatism decrease our internal pranic flow and hide its gifts.

Q: What if an individual definitely doesn't believe in the idea of God?

A: Provided they can accept the idea of an infinitely loving and nurturing field of universal intelligence that is everywhere – within us and around us – then that will suffice. Being educated into this field's gifts and the power of prana as cosmic particles is important as it opens up fields of possibility. The Prana Program is about mind over matter and how much love a person is open to and can attract, hold and radiate and these do not need the "God reality" to exist.

Q: What about someone who is a staunch Christian?

A: Provided they are open to all the gifts that come to a person who is fully immersed in Christed consciousness then this is not a limitation. Zinaida Baranova, the Russian Breatharian, achieved this state purely through her devotion to Christ.

Q: You claim The Prana Program can unify the world's religions. How?

A: When we increase our pranic flow it floods us with an experience of pure Divine Love which allows us to move from purely intellectual religious perspectives and dogma. This flow of love is something any person who breathes can experience regardless of religious or cultural conditioning hence it can provide a common unifying bond as the same force sustains us all regardless of how we label it. Some metaphysicians say we are all cells existing in the body of one supremely loving and wise organism. As The Prana Program focuses on understanding field science then it doesn't matter what people call their God.

Q: Is there an international organization of pranic nourishers and if so what is its agenda? Is it a cult or religious movement?
A: No and no. Personally speaking, being a pranic nourisher is two per cent of who I am and is something that I, and others in the west, are happily pioneering due to the potentially powerful and positive global ramifications.

Q: Still many people do call you a "guru" or the leader of the breatharian cult. How do you respond to this?
A: There is only one guru people need and that is the Divine One Within. People are the masters of their own destiny and none are victims for we all create our own reality. Gurus are just experts or teachers in a particular esoteric field and the real guru teaches you to find the guru within. In this reality cults cannot exist for there are no leaders only masters.

Q: Can the lion really lay down with the lamb as per the Biblical prophecy of true peace among all kingdoms?
A: Again this is to do with the morphogenetic field. If we eliminate the aggressive nature of human kind and cease the slaughter of human and animal life, this will change the social and planetary biofield resonance powerfully enough to imprint all kingdoms. If we then ensure that all individuals are plugged in to energy channels that provide complete nourishment so that we all feel fulfilled and become altruistic, aware and begin to act like loving respectful masters; then obviously this too will also imprint all kingdoms. I have often said as I travel, that the level of aggression we see in the animal kingdom is a mirror of the level of aggression that we see in the human kingdom. Eliminate our human aggression, and boost our Divine Love radiation capacity, and we will see the 'lion laying down with the lamb' reality.

NOTE: for further Q & A's on Ascension and Enlightenment see Chapter 1.

THE PRANA PROGRAM
Enjoyable & Effective Evolution with Jasmuheen
e-book at http://www.selfempowermentacademy.com.au/htm/cia-education.asp#pranaprogram

---

PRANA AND THE ENVIRONMENT – Restoring balance and resources.

Q: How do you see The Prana Program effecting the environment?

A: I see The Prana Program impacting on the environment in a few stages and each stage will have the effect of restoring environmental balance and minimizing resource drainage.

Q: Can you describe these stages?

A: The first stage that we are now ready for is global vegetarianism and the grain saved on no longer feeding livestock will feed millions more each year; e.g. reduce the American meat intake by 10% and 60 million more can be fed. In 1961 the AMA said 90% of disease can be prevented by a vegetarian diet. Resource sustainability also depends on our taking the next step and becoming a vegetarian planet. As mentioned, global vegetarianism is Step 1 in the Pranic Nutrition Agenda. While our world – en mass – may not be ready for living solely on pranic nourishment, it is more then ready to adopt a global vegetarian reality and there are three main reasons for this to be now seriously considered:-

1. Vegetarianism improves health when understood and applied carefully.
2. More effective use of global resources with a softer impact on our environment.
3. It increases our global experience of kindness and compassion towards all life – human and animal.

Meat eaters use five times the resources compared to grain eaters in underdeveloped countries and 20 times the resources in the west. So in the west right now we can all begin to go vegetarian and make a huge difference immediately. We can also redirect what we save on food into social welfare programs and encourage resource redistribution. The farmers can begin to work with their DOW and find alternate means to survive economically that benefit the planet in a different way instead. A world free from senseless slaughter is an interesting goal.

I also stress vegetarianism as the next global step instead of pranic nourishment as all the research into its benefits have already been proven. Vegetarianism will make a huge difference immediately to our world and global pranic nourishment will come in its own time. As consciousness changes – we automatically become kinder and more compassionate and this will extend to the animal kingdom as well. Ethical economics will dominate in the future.

Q: Exactly how would global vegetarianism impact on our world's resources?

A: As the impact of this is so enormous we will share a list of specific research statistics in the final section of this book.

Q: What about The Prana Program's impact on food resources?
A: This is even more momentous and people can affect this immediately. By simply going from three meals a day to two people reduce their dependence on the world's food resources by 30% – or two meals to one by 50%. Choosing a prana only nourishment stream changes all of our environment pollution and resource drainage statistics phenomenally.

Q: Why are you so insistent on global vegetarianism being the next evolutionary stage?
A: In my book *Ambassadors of Light* we took the pranic discussion to the global stage and shared how societies must keep evolving, not just for the good of a few but for the good of the whole. Most typewriters have been made redundant by computers which offer superior benefits, the horse and buggy was quickly replaced by the motor car and we have come a long way since men rode on horseback as couriers to deliver mail. Now we have electronic mail.

In terms of dietary choices I personally see that the consumption of meat, given what we now know, can be likened to delivering mail via horseback while living on light is equivalent to e-mail - no middle man required, just better technology.

According to Harvey Diamond, the presidents of the National Academy of Sciences, National Academy of Engineering and the Institute of Medicine jointly said: "We believe that global environmental change may well be the most pressing international issue of the next century."

The economic and resource effects of a prana only nourishment regime are staggering, as well as the impact on our environment, and cannot be ignored.

PRANA & POLITICS – Harmonizing the fields effectively.

Facts to repeat and note:-
- Because we live in fear, the monthly cost of keeping U.S.A troops in Iraq is US$4.1 billion (Harper's magazine 06/05).
- Cost to eliminate all global poverty is US$350 billion per annum. According to World Bank research, less than 1/3 of current world expenditure is spent on weapons of war which could be redirected annually to eliminate global poverty.

In metaphysics a common reality is that to harmonize a country, civilization or a world, we need to refine and harmonize the individual and their presence in the community and global fields.

Refining an individual so that their presence is nourishing for all means also making sure that the refinement process is done in a way that is harmonious to all fields i.e. the game of harmony and self mastery must be aligned.

Q: So how does this apply to politics?

A: Thankfully this process of refinement can now be measured via a system of calibration as per the insights offered in David Hawkins's book *Power vs. Force*. Hence it is our recommendation that neither individuals, communities nor countries with a calibration less than 500, be allowed to lead or influence world affairs. E.g. as the energy of truth and integrity calibrates at 200, openness and willingness at 310, and wisdom at 400, then we recommend that a presidential candidate must calibrate at 540+ which is the energy of unconditional love and also that all political candidates and advisors must calibrate at 500+. This means they will be operating lovingly and wisely beyond power and ego based agendas.

Q: How about using this system to make the U.N. and other similar organizations more effective?

A: Precisely. For example, only when a country has a collective calibration of 500 can they interfere or add to the global political, evolutionary guidance game. Countries with a calibration of 300+ can contribute resource aid to other countries but they must do so unconditionally and without political strings although governments receiving the aid must distribute it to the needy and not line their own personal bank accounts – nonetheless if only those of a 500+ calibration can lead then this will not be an issue. In other words, this recommendation means that we clean up our own back yard before interceding in another's.

Part of The Prana Program's agenda is to offer a holistic education package that increases personal, community and global calibration levels so that field harmony is increased and health and hunger challenges are addressed and dealt with effectively. The Prana Program also offers effective ways of measuring these changes using the testing tools already given.

Q: How would you then fund this type of holistic education package?

A: Funding for the type of holistic packages that share the 8 point Luscious Lifestyle Program will come from:-
1) the money saved on declining health care needs as people get healthier,
2) from less spent on food production as people are fed in different ways and

3) also by the savings on the creation of weapons of war as people live in greater inner then outer peace with less fear. We can then redirect the money saved on global disarmament to meeting basic human rights as discussed in detail in my book *Ambassadors of Light – World Health, World Hunger Project.*

Additional note: As the fields don't lie, and as we are all interconnected, then the tools for testing calibrations can be used in many advantageous ways. E.g. any environmental, political, religious and even aid agencies agendas can be tested and if found to be calibrating at less then 200, they can be discarded or refined until their calibration levels improve and become more harmonious. Anything less than 200 definitely needs addressing.

Q: How does increasing the pranic flow change political perspectives?
A: It expands consciousness and gives greater mental clarity, more common insight and increased compassion; and decreases ego based, greed based and power based agendas.

Q: Shouldn't spiritual realities be kept separate from politics?
A: Religion and politics have often been bed mates and The Prana Program will promote harmony and unity through all levels of society thus influencing all decision makers to operate for the greater good of all.

All life is political as we constantly negotiate our way through it. All life is spiritual as we weave our way through the fields learning and growing. In metaphysics everything is interwoven and impacts upon the whole and nothing is separate.

Q: Since 1998 you have been promoting different ways to convert to pranic nourishment and no longer support the 21 day process. Why?
A: I felt that as a leading vocal proponent of The Prana Program, it needed to be offered as safely as possible with the best education regarding its total gifts with less emphasis on just the nourishment aspect. Hence we wrote, *The Food of Gods*. Also 70% of people undergoing the 21 day process choose to ignore the guidelines in the book thus potentially risking their health and needlessly damaging my reputation and polluting the true message of The Prana Program.

Q: But with this Prana Program book, you are now back to the nourishment aspects, why?

THE PRANA PROGRAM
Enjoyable & Effective Evolution with Jasmuheen
e-book at http://www.selfempowermentacademy.com.au/htm/cia-education.asp#pranaprogram

A: As mentioned in the introduction, there has been so much focus again on the Africa situation, with BBC documentaries, the Live Aid concerts, forgiveness of Third World debt programs etc, and as I have witnessed all of this, I had to ask myself what we have achieved regarding global education with The Prana Program and also how it can be pragmatically applied in Third World countries.

Over the last decade since we first became public with this, so much has changed and we have all become much better informed and, since no-one else has stepped forward with this for Third World countries, I have decided to. In doing so I wanted to make a simple Q & A manual regarding prana and all of its attributes without going too much into the how's as we do in other manuals in The Divine Nutrition series.

Q: In what way have you become better informed?
A: I believe that we now understand more of the science of this prana program and that it can be applied quite simply and logically with positive results. For example, in 2003 I was in Romania sharing many of our tools and insights and when I returned there in 2005 I discovered that not only had people read all of my books but they had personally applied the tools given, seen great positive changes in their life, taught their family and friends the same tools and seen how they also had enjoyed great changes and then they all came back for more. It was so heartwarming and inspirational for me to deal with people who were so open to a good re-education program and who would and did apply the teachings experientially with great results. All of this has inspired me to take it all now into Third World countries having had the success we have had with our work in the Eastern Bloc countries as it seems that when countries have experienced great loss or repression they are much more eager for positive tools for change.

THE PRANA PROGRAM
Enjoyable & Effective Evolution with Jasmuheen
e-book at http://www.selfempowermentacademy.com.au/htm/cia-education.asp#pranaprogram

෴ 7 ෴

Q & A's on the 21 day process, Skeptics & The Media

If I was launching The Prana Program newly into the world, I would not include the following chapter as it deals with some of the problems of our past. However I feel that once this current program is launched, that from time to time it may also need to address any old conceptual ideas and misinformations that others may hold so that the path of misconception can be illumined and cleared.

THE PRANA PROGRAM AND THE 21 DAY PROCESS

Q: In your first book on The Prana Program, you describe not just your personal experience with this conversion but also a specific initiation now known as the 21 day process. Briefly, what was the 21 day process initiation about?
A: It was a spiritual initiation that increased our internal light quotient and personal calibration levels and as a consequence delivered to some people the gift of being able to be free from the need to take physical food. For some it recalibrated us into deeper levels of the Divine Love channel so that we could receive other esoteric gifts.

Q: What motivated you to do the 21 day process?
A: At that time my only interest was in my personal ascension and path of enlightenment. If someone had said, "do this initiation and you won't need to take physical food anymore", it would not have interested me. Living purely on prana for physical nourishment was a small by-product of a much bigger personal, spiritual journey, that is still unfolding. To me enlightenment is a journey not a destination, as we can always increase our capacity to attract and radiate more light.

Q: What were the benefits you gained from undergoing the 21 day initiation?
A: This is hard to say as my general lifestyle at the time kept me in the channels where many gifts came so it's hard to separate them. However I believe the 21 day process accelerated and expanded my capacity for things such as being constantly in the flow of Grace, experiencing constant synchronicity, inter-dimensional telepathy, clairsentience and also the prana as nourishment reality.

THE PRANA PROGRAM
Enjoyable & Effective Evolution with Jasmuheen
e-book at http://www.selfempowermentacademy.com.au/htm/cia-education.asp#pranaprogram

Q: What are its problems or challenges?

A: If a person is unprepared and not listening to their inner voice there can be many problems with the 21 day process, from extreme weight loss to even loss of their life. An athlete must train to compete with ease in a marathon and it is similar with the 21 day initiation – people need to be physically, emotionally, mentally and spiritually fit so that they have the right calibration levels.

Q: You constantly share that you prefer the conversion process detailed in **The Food of Gods** *book, why?*

A: It is a slower and safer system of conversion that promotes easier integration within the physical, emotional and mental bodies. It eliminates many of the problems that people had with the 21 day process.

Q: Such as?

A: The 21 day process is a fast track program that switches people too quickly from one reality to another. There is not much social/family/emotional body adjustment time so it can be a shock to the bio-system on these levels. A gradual process of refinement seems to lessen this and be more permanent.

Q: Would everyone doing the 21 day process be aiming to connect with the higher or ascended aspect of their divine nature?

A: No. 83% of people surveyed throughout the globe, said they did the 21 day process because it just felt right; 72% did it to experience their God – the DOW. 19% did it for health reasons and 12% for dietary reasons and 5% out of curiosity! But I say to people: "If you don't believe in God, or the U.F.I.*, then if you stop eating what do you think is going to feed you?" To do this one needs to know they create their own reality and also have mind mastery such as "I expect prana, the God force, to feed me", and so it does as the U.F.I. mirrors and supports our beliefs.
* U.F.I. = Universal Field of infinite love and Intelligence.

Q: In your first book on this the steps that people needed to undertake to prepare for the program were quite simple, but in your later books the instructions have become more detailed e.g. vegetarian for several years, vegan for six months and raw food and liquid for a further six months. Why is this?

A: I came from a background of over 20 years of physical fitness, vegetarian diet, meditation etc and I just assumed that anybody who would be attracted to this process would have naturally had that sort of background as well. For the untuned person the prana only program is a very extreme thing to do and one obviously needs to be well prepared for it to be as successful as it can be and to get the most out of it. So the new methods deal with more prolonged preparation and we now recommend that people convert their bodies into pranic nourishment via the program offered in the book *The Food of Gods* and also understand the cosmic particle hydration and feeding reality that we cover in *The Law of Love* manual with its emphasis also on heart energy.

Succinctly on just a dietary level if you wish to be a lot healthier and even be free from the need to eat food, then you first:-

- ☐ Become a vegetarian.
- ☐ Then become a vegan and cease consuming all animal products.
- ☐ Then move on to raw food, then go to fruits.
- ☐ Then liquids, then prana.

The more gradually you make this dietary transition, the easier it will be to let go of your emotional body's addiction to the pleasure gained from eating a wide variety of foods. Simultaneously a person needs to tune themselves mentally and emotionally. But dietary refinement alone will not attract enough cosmic particles to you to remain healthy on a prana only regime.

Remember The Prana Program is not about eating or not eating, it's about establishing a very strong connection with the Divine One Within – our DOW. A very small by-product of this is that It will feed us if we choose not to take nourishment from food any more but without this connection what will feed us? This is definitely not about a new non-physical food diet.

Q: Do you feel now that the guidelines in the first book were wrong or misleading?

A: Not wrong; but I assumed people would be a little more discerning and I assumed and trusted that people understood the true message of the book and would be self responsible and well prepared.

Q: Could you describe what the true message of your first book is?

A: Its basic message is that it is possible to be nourished on *all* levels by another source of nutrition and that the Divine One Within us can do this if we choose to allow it to. Our message is also about the need for humankind to take responsibility for everything that is happening in their life right now, because their choices are affecting the planet. There is a lot we can all do to make our transition through this new millennium a joyous one for all while utilizing resources more effectively. The first book was really the journey of my personal experience with this reality field and the realization that it is possible although I didn't understand the science of it and how. All I knew was that I was given the gift of this as a by-product of the 21 day initiation.

Q: So presumably only a few people would have the mind mastery and the physical fitness to go through the 21 day process discussed in your first book?
A: Or the desire. Still there are enough out there to create a global shift around this. A funny thing happens when people get information that's right for their blueprint – their heart sings. By asking, we can trigger a 'data download' of the blueprint as to why we're truly here. So if the information in the books on this subject doesn't make your heart sing, don't do it as it's not part your blueprint. If you decide to do it then you need to ask for help from the Divine One Within, so that the transition is one of joy and ease and grace, and then you need to clean up your diet, get fit, look at your emotions around food, and prepare your family. ONLY your DOW can provide the perfect conversion procedure for you and only your DOW can reveal to you your blueprint.

Q: You then took this "prana as nourishment" discussion to the Global stage with Book 2 in the Divine Nutrition series. What was its focus?
A: In book two *Ambassadors of Light – World Health, World Hunger Project*; we have more information regarding our research projects and we also emphasize again the need for fitness and preparation. Every edition that we have released we have added more information as we ourselves have been exposed to more and in this book we also applied it to Global programs such as resource redistribution, global environmental impact and other more political issues.

Q: You say in your additional material that not all people improve their health with the 21 day process and in fact some people's condition deteriorates?
A: It affects everyone differently although 91% of people surveyed said they found the 21 day process beneficial and 66% said their health improved. The initiation is about a redirection of energy and there are many gifts that happen to people through the 21 day process that are nothing to do with prana as an ongoing source of physical nourishment. I have noticed that the gifts people receive are dependant upon the purity of their intention.

Q: Did you put restrictions on who can do the 21 day process initiation, to make it safe?
A: You can't do that – it's out there, like a runaway train as the first book in the Divine Nutrition series is now in 17 languages, nonetheless we have released regular updates and guidelines, one

being "Get fit for Prana". We have also given out a checklist of what we want people to do and we keep updating and disseminating our research and recommendations. I take the view that people are intelligent and do use their discernment. Also we have the greatest teacher and guide with this which is the Divine One Within and It has our best interests at heart. Who am I to tell people what they can or can't do – particularly the sort of people who are pre-programmed to do this? But we can offer guidelines and improve our models with subsequent texts as we have continually done through our writings in the free online magazine The ELRAANIS Voice and now in this compendium.

Q: Can people who are sick do the 21 day process?

A: I hear about lots of miraculous healings occurring through increasing the pranic flow and yet many of these people are not fit on all levels yet still have found great benefit in doing this. Why The Prana Program heals some and not others we don't know but we do know that the fitter we are on all levels, the safer the 21 day process is. Still I personally recommend that everyone apply *The Food of Gods* conversion program instead.

THE PRANA PROGRAM – SKEPTICS AND THE MEDIA

Q: In 2000 you were awarded the IgNobel Prize for Literature by Harvard University for the Pranic Nourishment book, what was your response to this?

A: German philosopher, Arthur Schopenhauer said: "All truth passes through three stages. First, it is ridiculed. Second, it is violently opposed. Third, it is accepted as being self-evident." So good holistic education programs that focus on human potential and combine ancient eastern tradition will alleviate this. Having said this, my personal reaction to the news of the IgNobel Prize was lots of laughter as I'm sure the award was issued in good humor based on the seemingly incredulous nature of our reality.

Q: How do you now deal with skeptics?

A: Light-heartedly and with humor plus a dose of re-educational data. Things are rarely as they seem. For example, my favorite physical exercise lately is barefoot backward beach walking. Some who see me do this each day may think: "There goes that strange lady in the cowboy hat with no sunglasses, walking backwards again. I wonder if she's eccentric or does it for a reason?"

The hat shields my face from the hot Australian sun, yet wearing no sunglasses (which is unusual in our climate) allows me to absorb more prana directly into the brain through the eyes.

Walking barefoot means I can feed off ground prana and walking backwards rebalances my whole internal energy flow and energizes and exercises the body in a different way.

Similarly people say: "That's rubbish everyone has to eat, she's a liar". What they have not understood – due to lack of educational exposure – is all the benefits we discuss in this book, so you need to treat skepticism respectfully and lightly and humor always helps.

Q: Speaking of skeptics and doubt, you've been criticized for not doing empirical tests to prove your claims that prana nourishes you. Is this something you would be prepared to do?

A: I have done lots of allopathic and alternate testing to satisfy myself that it is possible as my body has remained healthy and I have shared the outcomes of this with the world. I have also worked with and been tested by doctors in Germany, India and more recently Russia. Due to the time I have needed to fulfill my own blueprints, I have not been prepared to interfere with my work schedule and get tested every time someone asks me to prove this. I also know that in time, as more people discover this, then prana power will prove itself and become a very common lifestyle choice for many – just as vegetarianism is today. Time is a good leveller in fields of controversy.

Q: As a leading proponent in the world for the Divine Nutrition paradigm, and as someone who has had to deal with all the natural skepticism regarding the pranic nourishment reality, what else do you see as the future of this?

A: Like many yogis and shaman, I have been blessed with the ability to glimpse – from time to time – into our future and I have witnessed that due to its personal and global benefits, the 'prana as nourishment' reality is being Divinely supported and will not go away. I have seen a world where the slaughter of any life – human or animal – is no longer part of our reality and is seen as something belonging to our more barbaric, unenlightened past. In this 'new' world, there is love, honor and respect for all life and people have been educated as to how to create and maintain physical, emotional, mental and spiritual fitness. In this world we exist in rainbow cities of crystalline light that radiate with love and wisdom and health and happiness.

The question is how do we get there?

What steps do we need to take to evolve into this new world?

The answer is simply a matter of the expansion of our consciousness which happens when we adopt a more holistic lifestyle that is designed to change our brain wave patterns and activate our higher sensibilities.

While skepticism is healthy, ignorance and fear come from lack of education which is why it is crucial for those in the 'frontlines' of this new paradigm, to always act as masters. Part of this mastery entails being able to hold and radiate the vibration of love in all situations regardless of what is happening.

Q: How has the media dealt with this reality in the west?

A: Generally it has been very supportive although in my personal experience the mainstream media has often been more focused on sensationalism than responsible educational reportage. Also while I appreciate the fact that they wish to present two viewpoints, asking someone who is completely ignorant as to the prana field, questions about its possibilities, so that the media can offer an objective view is very strange to me. We have done over a decade of experiential research with thousands on this and to ask us questions and then check it with a medical practitioner who often hasn't even heard of prana, who operates in Beta field mentality, all of this is also very nonsensical to me. It's like asking a mathematician to comment on the complexities of writing a symphony of music – different field of education and creativity.

Q: At the start of the millennium you virtually retired from dealing with global mainstream media regarding education with The Prana Program. Why?

A: Firstly we had completed the anchoring of this reality in the morphogenetic field by imprinting nearly one sixth of Earth's population with the reality of this possibility. This gave me the luxury of being able to be a lot more selective and only deal with open and positive media of integrity. Most proponents of this program retire from mainstream media after a while as the sensationalistic stand the media often adopt can be a little disconcerting. Secondly it was time for me to begin another level of my own service blueprint.

Q: As media spokesperson you now have spoken – directly or indirectly – to over 1 billion people about Divine Nutrition since 1997, what has been your greatest learning in dealing with a disbelieving and skeptical media?

A: Most of what I have learnt regarding dealing with the mainstream skeptical media I outlined in the document on Responsible Reporting at:-
http://www.selfempowermentacademy.com.au/htm/files/docs/DNP-RESPONSIBLE-REPORTING.pdf

I have personally learnt greater humility and also that when we stand in a truth, that is a real experience for us, then it doesn't matter what people say. I have also learnt the benefits and importance of good research and thorough knowledge – both intellectual and experiential – of a subject. Lastly I experienced a reconfirmation that research that is beneficial for the world is not necessarily promoted if it clashes with more dominant money or power agendas. The economic, environmental and medical changes that will eventually occur through the adoption of The Prana Program are revolutionary and so can only come via a change in human consciousness where win/win/win resolutions are supported.

Q: Why have you persisted in being vocal with The Prana Program?

A: Because the benefits that The Prana Program offers to our world are too amazing and positive to ignore. I have also persisted in dealing with selective media as I believe it is one of our most powerful tools for speeding up global education and releasing the world from both fear and ignorance paradigms – assuming of course that it is used for the highest good and in integrity.

Q: There have been a few deaths associated with this 21 day process – can you elaborate on these?

A: As I was not directly involved with this I can only provide data from what I have been told as I researched this and I have never been given the full facts of any of the cases. I would like to add that those were also fully investigated by relevant police bodies that cleared me of all culpability. The controversy stems not because people have died but because people don't believe it is possible to do this so therefore to them, for me to suggest it is possible is morally wrong and people ivolved are being misled. Provided it is not somebody's exit time and provided they have prepared responsibly by fine-tuning their systems and their calibration, then living purely on prana is not only safe but improves our health and longevity levels.

While I personally would have preferred no loss of life in association with this, and that everyone acted responsibly, the following facts cannot be ignored:-

   a) Metaphysically you cannot die unless it is your time. Your DOW and the U.F.I. will circumvent an untimed death. David Hawkins's calibration research shares that we know the exact time of our death the moment we are born.
   b) The issue that so many people die from lack of proper nourishment needs to be immediately addressed. Statistically we can lose 3 in 20,000 over the period of a decade, or one every 2 seconds from starvation, so we need to see a different perspective on this.

People die constantly from lack of medical expertise, from incorrect diagnosis, ignorance of underlying causative factors and more. All of this can be rebalanced and lessened via The Prana Program's lifestyle for preventative medicine. Car accidents and sedentary lifestyles, war and famine, plus misuse of prescription drugs will kill billions more people than an irresponsible conversion to The Prana Program ever will; e.g. "There are over 10 million adverse reactions yearly from FDA-approved over-the-counter and prescriptions drugs. We are not talking about mild nausea or headaches. Between 60,000 and 140,000 people die each year from adverse drug reactions. Each year, more Americans die after taking prescription drugs than died in the entire Vietnam war." Julian Whitaker, M.D. Author of *Reversing Heart Disease, Guide to Natural Healing,* and other books.

Q: After the death of the woman in Scotland you were challenged by Australian "60 Minutes" to undergo a period of 7 days with no food and no fluid – what was the outcome of this trial apart from what the mainstream media reported?

A: The outcome was that "60 Minutes" stopped the experiment after 5 days fearing I would be successful which could create problems for them as their intention was always to portray me as deluded and also for them to prove that going without food or fluid is dangerous which it is for the unprepared. The outcome was set by them before we began (although I was naïvely not aware of their intention) so it was always deemed to be seen as a failure. Calibration testing will attest to this as it is all unbiasedly recorded in the U.F.I.

Q: What did you learn from this "60 Minutes" challenge?

A: Personally I learnt not to be so naïve and trusting in journalistic integrity. I also learnt to only be involved in experiments with well informed people who have positive intentions and the best interest of global education at heart and who share the same level of integrity.

I also realized that you cannot underestimate the intelligence of the audience who when asked for their input on the program that covered my story, initially 70% said that they believed it was possible, a result of support for this that astounded both myself and the "60 Minutes" team.

Q: If you could wind back time, would you do it again?

A: Yes. I choose to see everything as perfect as all situations have some gift of learning to impart, however I would refine and legalize the agreements to avoid incorrect reporting and "60 Minutes" backing out and add unbiased validation from detached parties who are motivated by higher paradigms.

Q: So do you believe that any publicity – good or bad – is beneficial?

A: Not always, nonetheless even if it is less than supportive, publicity on this issue at least plants seeds of thought in people's minds and those seeds can blossom into the light of understanding with further education.

Q: You said earlier that it is hard to track how many people in the west now utilize The Prana Program, is that because of negative social reaction?
A: On one level yes. Due to how challenging this paradigm is to mainstream reality, many of us have already lived through both ridicule, plus overt and covert opposition, yet we know that eventually The Prana Program will come into a state of acceptance. As these stages unfold in the different countries where the light eaters are demonstrating this paradigm, some have gone underground rarely speaking of such things, others are very public in their support but most are simply circumspect, relying on their inner guidance as to whom they can share such things with.

Q: Since you are semi-retired from mainstream media is there anyone else who has picked up the gauntlet regarding being so public with The Prana Program?
A: Yes, the bringers of change always work in waves:- in the 1970's Wiley Brooks launched 'breatharianism' into the American scene, then I held the very public position with 'pranic nourishment' in Australia, Asia and Europe for nearly a decade until I completed my media assignment with this work. Then Hira Ratan Manek became the public face as he relentlessly toured in India and the U.S.A, and worked with the various medical and science teams to offer his research and experience with the 'solar feeding' program.

After Hira there will be someone else and so it will continue. And of course we recognize all the work that others have done to contribute personally and professionally to the anchoring of this reality. You can tell when a paradigm is here to stay when many different people, from many different backgrounds, most who have never met, start to reach and share the same findings and one of the current excitements within esoteric circles is regarding the gifts that come when we consciously shift brain wave patterns and work with the energy of love and compassion which are also two important aspects for success with The Prana Program.

Q: You also stress the need for honesty every step of the way with this conversion process why?
A: I have seen the wonderful work of a number of people in this field discredited unnecessarily. For example there have been cases of well known light eaters who have relaxed with this over the years

and chosen to eat a meal now and then. When confronted with this they denied it and hence their reputation was ruined and their valuable work in this field discredited.

Being nourished by prana is not necessarily a black and white reality where we either eat regularly or never eat. To me it has always been about freedom of choice and honesty in our journey helps others appreciate this.

For example, not one cell of my body believes it needs food to be sustained or to live. Knowing that – both intellectually and experientially – I am at choice and without fear of negative consequences of whether I eat or not, it does not matter.

We need to remember that while living a prana only nourishment seems incredulous to others – due to the lack of education and exposure to this possibility – the only person we need to prove anything to is ourselves, this is our freedom journey and we need to be honest with ourselves and others to make the pathway easier and to honor the challenges we face along the way.

⊰ 8 ⊱

Solar Nourishment, Bigu & The Bigger Picture

SOLAR NOURISHMENT – QUESTIONS WITH HIRA RATAN MANEK

Q: What is Solar Nourishment?
A: Solar nourishment is the flow of pure prana through our sun from the inter-dimensional Central sun where its frequencies are stepped down to a radiation that Earth and her inhabitants can handle. It is a diffused form of pure Christed consciousness where Christed means pure Divine Love. Channelled directly into the brain through the eyes, it stimulates brainwave changes and activates the higher brain centers as well as nourishing the body. Leading proponent of Solar Nourishment is Hira Ratan Manek and his website www.solarhealing.com has more details and we offer a Solar Nourishment program in the next section. Hira has been involved in medical and scientific research on this and below are some of the findings with Dr Shah.

Q: There are substantial differences between how Hira – HRM – and you access and utilize The Prana Program. Can you elaborate on this?
A: The main difference between our systems is that the solar nourishment system is primarily an alternate external feeding system that obtains pure prana through the sun. The system I have been researching is an internal feeding system that accesses violet light as cosmic particles using the energy centers of our chakras and also working with the atoms. Over the last few years we have been testing this by spending periods of time in a darkroom environment that has been devoid of physical food and any external light. This has allowed us to experience more powerfully a natural inner light flow and also to feel the effects of the brain's increase in the production of melatonin plus the neuro-hormones DMT and 5-MeO-DMT.

Q: The idea of Solar feeding or Surya-Yoga is all well and good but what about when we live in places where there is minimal sun and also maximum pollution that screens out beneficial pranic rays, like Europe in a long winter for example?
A: This is precisely why I feel that solar feeding principles alone are insufficient to sustain the Divine Nutrition flow en mass and that to do this we have to feed from the Central Sun's energy that flows

through our atoms from the inner universes. Also all successful solar feeders that I have met including Hira Ratan Manek practice their version of the 8 point Luscious Lifestyles Program as discussed previously. In order to consistently maintain our health and happiness levels, we must consciously manage our internal and external energy flow and keep our calibration at certain levels.

Note from Jasmuheen: Hira once said to me that the energies coming through the physical sun are so powerful that as they flow into our bodies through the eyes they flood our system and burn off any dross, hence purifying and nourishing us regardless of our belief systems. During 2005 Hira returned to occassionally taking small amounts from food as his busy service schedule meant less exposure to sunlight and barefoot walking practices. Unsure of whether to share this publically or not, he remained silent but was discovered by others who were angered at his initial denials. I sincerely hope that all his wonderful work is not discounted because of this incident.

Data from Dr Shah's research on HRM: When HRM was tested over a 411 day period under strict constant supervision. Full document at:

http://www.selfempowermentacademy.com.au/pdf/light-ambassadry-research-booklet.pdf

Drawing energy from Cosmic Sources, Dr Shah sees solar feeding as energy mathematics rather than calorie mathematics. He says:-

"Out of all cosmic sources, the SUN is the most powerful and readily available source and has been used for energy, by sages and Rishis since ancient time, including Lord Mahavir, Tibetan lamas and other Rishes. Again, how the SUN energy is received – the Brain and the mind are the most powerful recipients in human body, the retina and the pineal gland (the third eye or the seat of soul as per Rene Descartes) are equipped with photoreceptor cells and may be considered photosensitive organs. As plant kingdom thrives on chlorophyll and photosynthesis, directly dependant on the Sun, similarly some photosynthesis must be taking place when we hypothesize Sun energy."

Q: How does this sun energy enter the body?

Answer from Dr Shah's research: "Through complex ways and distinct. There is a pathway from the retinas, to the hypothalamus, called the retinohypothalamic tract. This brings information about the dark and light cycles to suprachiasmatic nucleus (SCN) of the hypothalamus. From the SCN, impulses along the nerve travel via the pineal nerve (Sympathetic nerves system) to the pineal gland. These impulses, inhibit the production of Melatonin. When these impulses stop (at night or in dark, when the light no longer stimulates the hypothalamus) pineal inhibition ceases, and Melatonin is released. The pineal gland (or the third eye) is therefore a photosensitive organ and an important timekeeper for the human body. The unexplored process of energy synthesis and transformation from the sun energy perhaps partly occurs here."

Q: What have you discovered about the pineal gland's role in this?
Answer from Dr Shah's research: "While going through the details of recent scientific literature and also comparing it with ancient Indian spiritual texts, as well as western occult and new age, the following things are apparent. The activation of pineal gland is the key step in psychic, spiritual and energy transformation processes. Here in this gland, energy processing and re-distribution occurs. Pineal gland is the commander of all endocrine glands, therefore controlling the humeral system. It also regulates the circadian rhythm, sleep wake cycle and it also slows down ageing process. It has psychic properties and is the seat of soul or mind – so called the third eye. It is the Agna (Ajna) chakra of tantric system. Its activation can be done with prolonged yoga and meditation techniques or through practice of solar energy. The later does not use classic yoga steps. Pineal also inhibits growth and metastasis of some tumors. It has a stimulatory effect on the immune system."
Thank you Dr Shah.

BIGU & QIGONG

Q: What about the state of Bigu that the Qigong masters talk about? What is this?
A: Bigu is the state that a person can enter into spontaneously from the practice of qigong, it is a state where they are free from the need to take physical food and sometimes also fluid. "*Bigu* is a state in which a person maintains a normal life without taking any food. Standard *Bigu* means very little or no intake of water. Basic *Bigu* means only drinking water and juice. Non-standard *Bigu* means ingesting water, juice and occasionally juicy fruits and vegetable soups."

While I have personally experienced all three states of Bigu by choice over the last 12 years, as the work of these Qi masters is focused on other areas of health, they discourage publicity about Bigu as they feel society is not ready to accept the Bigu phenomena.

Q: Can you share some more about qigong?
A: The website http://www.qigong.net/ shares: "A long time ago in ancient China, people gradually realized through their struggle for survival that certain body movements, mental concentration and imagination, along with various ways of breathing, could help them to adjust some body functions. This knowledge and experiences were summarized and refined with time, and passed down through generations ... shaping what is known today as the Traditional Qigong.

"A common characteristic of qigong is the simultaneous training of the body and the mind. The dual cultivation of personality and essence is the main content of traditional qigong. Its style consists of both movements and stillness, and its method is characterized by the combination of the mind (consciousness), Qi (bio-energy), the body, and the spirit.

"Traditional Qigong is based on the principle of Virtue. Only by emphasizing virtue, being virtuous, and maintaining virtue, and with benign virtuous heart, virtuous character, and virtuous action can we achieve harmony with our surroundings and meet the three required states for practicing qigong: calm, tranquil, and natural. Virtue is the golden key to enter the gate of qigong." A virtuous life is also the key for increasing the pranic flow.

Q: You say that the qigong community have done a lot of research into Bigu, can you provide more data on this?

A: Yes, on page 286 in the book *Scientific Qigong Exploration* by nuclear physicist Lu Zuyin, he shares further about the state of *Bigu* and also about the experiments conducted on people who have not eaten for up to 6 years. Dr Yan Xin is one of the most respected and widely recognized Qi masters in China and it is with his co-operation that in-depth studies have been conducted and shared with the world. Many people have spontaneously entered into the Bigu state as a result of being in his presence, and much research has been documented in the Chinese language. In fact over sixty books have been written covering his research into the power and benefits of Qi emissions.

Q: Is there a common calorie intake level between the pranic nourishers that you know and the Bigu practitioners?

A: According to the scientists measuring qigong emissions and studies on the Bigu state, many people in Bigu live on less than 300 calories per day for years without any damage to their physical bodies. In October 1987 Ding Jing, aged 10, went into the Bigu state and stayed there for over 6 years with a calorie intake of between 260 and 300 per day. We have found the same and many continue to live very healthily on calorie intakes that are continuing to defy and challenge modern medical and scientific belief. Personally I have become healthier through the Bigu states and have long ago proved to myself beyond doubt that some other power is nourishing my body.

Q: What do you feel is the main requirement to live purely on prana, what is the secret to living only on Divine Light?

A: After over a decade of personal experiential research and interviewing hundreds who live successfully via Divine Nutrition, my one conclusion is that it is our vibration that determines our success with this, nothing more, nothing less. Our vibration allows us to draw this nutrition from the inner planes and back through our cellular structure, if this is our intention. It also allows us to attract increased doses of both internal and external chi, or prana – in the form of a greater influx of Cosmic Fire, Akasha and Astral Light – which are the main elements sustaining all life particles. Things like a pure heart, the ability to serve with compassion and kindness, the openness to the Higher Laws and to using our higher mind, all these tune us powerfully to the channels that can reveal our paranormal powers, of which the ability of Bigu is just a small by-product.

Q: Apart from the explanations already given regarding how to attract more prana to the body and why this happens i.e. calibration, brain wave patterns etc, is there any other understanding in the Chinese research as to how this is possible particularly with healing and Bigu?

Answer with Eltrayan: Regarding how external prana can cause healing and a Bigu state, it is suggested that the average person has about 14-15 billion brain cells, but usually uses only 4-5% and never more than 30% of these cells. Even though as people age, they have memory failure, 80-90% of their brain cells remain unused at the time of their death. It has been observed that after a person enters into a state of exposure to external prana the neutrons in the deep layers of the cerebrum also enter into an excited state. This affects the regions of the brain where consciousness is focused. As a result the bio-electric currents in these regions are likely to be further enhanced. In other words, pranic practice activates the unused 80-90% of the brain cells by strengthening the brain's bio-electric currents.

On entering a pranic state the consumption of oxygen decreases while at the same time the lungs' ability to absorb oxygen increases. As well, the capacity of tissues in the whole body to store oxygen and the capacity of the lungs is enhanced. Consequently, pranic practice is much more effective than athletic training. A long distance runner has lungs with large capacities, but also consumes large amounts of oxygen, and as a result cannot stay under water for very long. However, some people are able to stay alive while being buried underground in a coffin for 6 to 7 days. It is difficult to explain this phenomenon according to the lung capacity and oxygen needs of an ordinary person. However, it is explainable from a pranic perspective. In a pranically enhanced state a practitioner does not need much oxygen. Pranic practices increase inhaling efficiency and expand the storage capacity of the lung tissues. It also decreases the consumption of oxygen.

Q: How is this possible? Are there any studied reasons that you have not already covered?

Answer with Eltrayan: Research shares that at certain stages of practice some pranic practitioners eat very little, or do not eat all. This is because they are capable of transforming energy and making full use of stored energy to keep themselves alive. A few do not even drink water, for water can be absorbed through the skin pores. One may question how a person can live without food. First, the gastric and internal fluid of pranic practitioners contain many nutrients. Second, everyone has nutrients stored in the body, yet most people do not know how to transform and utilize them. Many days may pass without eating food, yet one can still be energized by absorbing self transformed high energy substances. It is not a question of eating, but rather of absorbing nutrients in a different manner. One can utilize the body's accumulated nutrition and transfer it to gastric and intestinal fluids for high quality nourishment.

Pranic practitioners do not merely absorb nutrients through their mouth and nose. They can use many other ways to absorb energy substances for nourishment. Water, for example, does not have to enter only through the mouth. Light does not have to enter only through the eyes. Pranic practitioners absorb high energy substances from the universe that are unavailable to others. In this manner one can eat less or not eat at all for a length of time and still maintain a high energy level. When the absorption of high energy substances is enhanced, one may go without food for a long period of time. Thus pranic practices are an ideal way to improve the digestive system of the body.

Only the earliest of scientific research has been done to date on the amazing possibilities that pranic practices offer. However, the Chinese are the leaders in this field, and ten years of their research is now being translated into English books which will be very educational for western science. *(And perfect to apply to Third World countries to decrease health and hunger challenges.)*

THE PRANA PROGRAM AND THE BIGGER PICTURE

Q: You have said that the idea of just being free from the need to take physical food, is not enough motivation for people on this journey and that people wishing to be involved with it need to be aware of the 'bigger picture'. Could you explain what you mean by this?

A: Humanity has been gifted with an amazing ability which is to re-discover, recognize, experience and demonstrate the God Force within. We have been programmed to demonstrate this Divine Force and be one with it, any time we choose – for on one level we operate like mini computers that are run by the same software as the Cosmic Computer called God. This Divine Force, or God, radiates Its nurturing love and light through our inner sun center to feed our chakras, and through our physical world sun, and It has the power to feed our cells by both internal and external means. However the remarkable thing is not to see a human being become free from the need to eat physical food, but to see a human being radiate such light and love that all are fed by their presence.

Q: Why have you decided to offer The Prana Program for Third World challenges in this book, surely this is something just for aid agencies?

A: I believe that the wider we spread our research and share its relevance to such challenges, the sooner it may be accepted. The benefits of this are not just for the chosen few and by educating widely at a grass roots level we can address the challenge on many levels. It may also inspire others – apart from those in aid agencies and the U.N. – to share the data here with appropriate channels that they know. I also believe that as more adopt this mental paradigm, it can be more powerfully holographically projected and imprinted into areas of need to change the field dynamics and soften the suffering.

Q: Is there anything else you would like to add to this discussion before we look at how The Prana Program can be applied to Third World aid programs?

A: Since we have just looked a little at Solar Nourishment, I think Mikhael Aivanhov summed it up best when he said: "When we focus our attention on the sun, the center of our universe, we draw closer to our own center, our higher self, the sun within; we melt into it more and more. But to focus our attention on the sun also means to learn to mobilize all our thoughts, desires and energies, and put them to work in the service of the highest ideal. He who works to unify the chaotic multitude of inner forces that constantly threaten to tear him apart, and launch them in the pursuit of one, luminous, beneficial goal, becomes a powerful focal point, capable of radiating in every direction.

"Believe me; a human being who masters the tendencies of his own lower nature can benefit the whole of mankind. He becomes as radiant as the sun. His freedom is such that his consciousness embraces the whole human race as he pours out the superabundance of light and love that dwell within him. The world needs more and more human beings capable of dedicating themselves to this work with the sun, for only love and light are capable of transforming humanity."

**We offer this next section as a way of eliminating
all health and hunger challenges in our world
although it is tailor made for Third World countries.**

ଓ 9 ଓ

The Prana Program

for World Health & Hunger Challenges

Specializing in Third World countries – to be used in conjunction with existing aid and resource redistribution programs.

Researched and written by Jasmuheen and the Cosmic Internet Academy, as presented to The Society for Conscious Living at the United Nations Building, Vienna November 2005, after 12 years of trial and error in the west among 20,000 people.

Go to www.selfempowermentacademy.com.au
for more Positive Planetary Paradigms

THE PRANA PROGRAM
Enjoyable & Effective Evolution with Jasmuheen
e-book at http://www.selfempowermentacademy.com.au/htm/cia-education.asp#pranaprogram

The Prana Program

Specifically addressing:
Third World Challenges

Intentions & Outcomes	144
Part a) Mental Attitudes & Mindsets	146
Part b) Community Life & Supportive Fields	152
Part c) Alternate Pragmatic Internal Feeding Mechanisms	157
Part d) A simple Solar Feeding Program, Bigu & Research	169
Part e) Resource Sustainability & Environmental Statistics	174
Part f) Resource Redistribution & The Prana Program	177

The Prana Program – eradicating health & hunger issues in all countries.

**THE PRANA PROGRAM POWERPOINT PRESENTATION with Jasmuheen –
http://www.jasmuheen.com/ezyedit/fileLib/Press/THE-PRANA-PROGRAM.htm**

*Minimizing Global Health & Hunger Challenges –
Data extract from THE PRANA PROGRAM e-book*

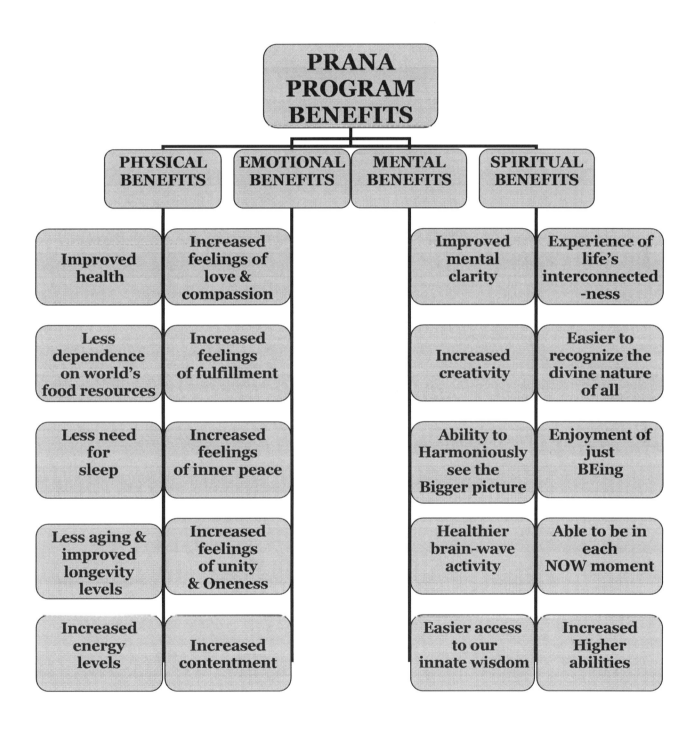

THE PRANA PROGRAM
Enjoyable & Effective Evolution with Jasmuheen
e-book at http://www.selfempowermentacademy.com.au/htm/cia-education.asp#pranaprogram

Introduction:- Intentions, outcomes and definitions.

Q: What is your intention with offering The Prana Program to Third World countries? What outcome would you like to achieve?

A: After 12 years of experiential research and refinement of this feeding system in the west, and with the continuing focus on providing more effective aid packages into countries like Africa, and Third World countries, we would like to add our research as an additional layer to the usual aid programmes. Using modern technology of the internet with audio and visual presentations, we can train people to understand and teach a simple program of alternate internal nutrition, and thus alleviate some of the stress of trying to distribute other resources into these areas.

We also hope to reduce mortality rates and pro-actively improve health and happiness levels of those struggling to survive who currently suffer from lack of proper nourishment. With a child dying of hunger related diseases every 2 seconds there is nothing to be lost and everything to be gained by adding The Prana Program to existing aid packages.

Q: Is it your intention that The Prana Program replace normal food supplies in all countries?

A: In the short term definitely not. However increasing the pranic flow, and adding the mindset that prana can provide an additional level of nourishment, can be very beneficial to all. For example, I know of many people who for years have lived very healthily without taking vitamin supplements and whose calorie intake has averaged less than 300 calories per day – myself included. By relying on prana to provide what we need nutritionally, our dependancy on global food resources has dropped substantially with no detriment to our health. For example, in a recent BBC documentary where people in Ethiopia were existing only on wild cabbage grass, when their food rations ran out, this would not be a problem if prana can supplement their diet until aid programmes were more effectively placed. In the long term the successful implementation of The Prana Program will eliminate the need for many external aid programmes.

Q: Wouldn't the correct implemenation of The Prana Program also affect the operational status of existing aid programs?

A: Yes definitely. Many aid programmes provide water and food and the means of cultivation of both. As community calibrations change and success is activated with the physical nourishment aspect of The Prana Program then we will see an improvement also in community health. Programs with an emphasis on farming and food production will change dramatically.

Q: How can this be most easily achieved?

A: In four ways.

1) Education to understand The Prana Program and the adoption of new mindsets;
2) Breathing techniques based on ancient proven practices;
3) The use of specific internal feeding mechanisms that magnetize an increased pranic flow to nourish and hydrate the physical system;
4) Community support to experience and support The Prana Program first hand;
5) Responsible media reportage to highlight the success and spread The Prana Program methodology.

Q: How do you propose The Prana Program be taught in Third World countries?

A: As this is a pioneering field we are obviously open to recommendations but suggest that it initially be trialed in one village so that adjustments to the model and success assessments can be made. Also with the simple Sway and Tummy Breath test tools people can self assess every step of the way although results will easily be evident by an increase in health and a decrease in mortality rates.

Initially we would also look at training within aid agencies using Audio/Visual and Powerpoint presentations as well as personal instruction regarding our research and tools.

The best teacher of this is obviously someone who is successfully living it and has proven personal results for they are individuals who are free of doubt and fear in this field.

THE PRANA PROGRAM
for 3rd World communities

So to apply The Prana Program to Third World countries, there are 3 areas we need to address:-

♥ Mental attitudes & mindsets

♥ Community life PLUS

♥ How to create & utilize alternate internal and external pranic feeding mechanisms including accessing solar micro food.

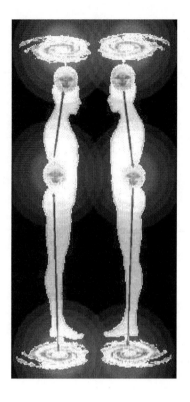

Part A:-
MENTAL ATTITUDES, MINDSETS & MISCELLANEOUS QUESTIONS

Introduction: One of the most important aspects of The Prana Program is education into the power of the human mind. This includes the proven power of positive thinking which research shares can increase a person's lifespan by 20% compared to those who consistently think negatively. Understanding also how to use our higher capabilities of brain power by creative visualization, will and intention, we can improve health and longevity levels in all countries and cultures. By combining mind mastery with ancient yogic practices and modern western research, we can re-educate all to the benefits of The Prana Program.

Q: How would you describe prana to a largely uneducated, Third World population?
A: Everyone has certain beliefs so we may need to find their terms to describe prana. For example, to the Christians we would describe prana as a nourishing aspect of the God force. For many it is not that difficult to understand that there is a force of energy that breathes us all, that loves us and that we can feel this love when we meditate upon it and that there is a force that guides us via our intuition.

With the acceptance of all of this, then the idea that this invisible force can also manufacture and deliver into our cells all the nutrition we need to be healthy and self regenerate, is not that difficult. Hopefully then we can also share the idea that this force can nourish us regardless of how much or how little we physically have to eat. With sound holistic education regarding the mind/body connection we can teach how to increase the flow of cosmic particles to our systems in a way that can feed us on all levels.

Q: How can The Prana Program be used as an alternate source of nourishment and hence be of benefit to underdeveloped Third World countries, or even to first world countries, that are suffering from lack of proper nourishment?

A: By the use of simple meditation tools, breath techniques and visualization procedures, we can instruct people how to nourish themselves from within and decrease their dependance on external food. This increases their self reliance and provides them with greater independence from the world's food resources and allows them to be nourished not just physically but also emotionally, mentally and spiritually.

Q: Surely people in Third World countries, or even First World countries, who are suffering from undernourishment firstly need access to good food and then education regarding healthy food choices?

A: Holistic education is required to break the cycles of poverty and good nourishment will simultaneously provide the strength to do it. Both go hand in hand. It is important to relieve people of the victim type consciousness that can accrue as they wait for the west to redistribute and deliver resources. The Prana Program allows for personal affirmative action.

Q: You talk in previous chapters about the need for people to have a particular calibration to safely exist on a prana only nourishment. How does this apply in Third World countries?

A: On one level it doesn't apply as the fact is that people are dying regardless, so The Prana Program may save lives that are already on the path to being lost, due to lack of availability of physical food, so we have nothing to lose and everything to gain by applying this program in Third World countries. In the west calibration levels apply to minimize unneccessary physical system damage.

Q: What about the spiritual reality of karma and souls choosing to incarnate into situations of starvation and poverty for their karmic learning and rebalancing?

A: In esoteric circles, it is well understood that people choose in each embodiment their culture, their parents, their race and the locality of their embodiment. Many believe that some people have entered into environments of poverty and suffering to complete karmic ties and chapters that have been unfinished from other lives. Regardless of this, many are very aware of the apathy that can come when one looks at the game of karma particularly regarding the caste system in India. It is easier to dismiss, and be inactive rather than active, by saying "It's their choosing – it is nothing to do with us".

Apathy separates, constructive compassion unifies.

Regardless of this, karmic learning can still be gained and energies rebalanced while living in a situation where basic human rights are met. As empathetic and aware adults we can work together to at least feed, clothe, shelter and holistically educate those open to this basic right. To do this is a sign of a civilized world.

Q: What about research into the field of solar nourishment?

A: As was discussed in detail in the previous chapter, Solar Nourishment is another way of gaining nutrition that we need by utilizing the sun's energy and absorbing this directly through our eyes into our brain which again stimulates the master glands and changes brain wave patterns. We will also share a simple solar nourishment program shortly.

Q: What has your research found regarding the role of our brain and our ability to be fed by prana or cosmic particles?

A: There are two levels to consider here.
   a) Physical brain stimulation and re-programming and using new software (specific mental commands) for the brain's computer to run, and
   b) Master gland activation and stimulation to change basic brain wave activity from Beta to Alpha to Theta.

When these are attended to we begin to utilize the $4/5^{th}$'s of the brain not normally used so we can tap into other levels of ability.

For example the below simple, mind mastery, energy directing tool was sent to me recently by a friend, she calls it:

"**Remembering how to produce manna:** Sit quiet, spine erect, breathe deeply and relax. Envision and connect with all of your glands – pituitary, pineal, thalamus, hypothalamus, parathyroid, thyroid, lymph, renal, all ethereal glands etc. – see them igniting, i.e. for instance see white light flashing out, or other images, just feel guided by your intuition. It does not matter if you do not know exactly where the glands in the body and your energy bodies are located. Just intend that your divine self and body will guide you and trust that everything will proceed as it should be. Then talk to your glands and set the intention by saying: "Thank you for producing manna now." Envision your spine and place this intent into the spine and then out through the nerves and their messaging system to the brain. Automatically your body produces manna. Repeat this technique as often as you need it and take as much time as you wish to ingest your manna."

This is another interesting tool to increase pranic flow that is based on mind power.

Q: Apart from what was discussed in earlier chapters of The Prana Program book, how does a person stimulate their brain to enhance their higher abilities e.g. use the 4/5th's not normally used?

A: One of the most effective ways is to flood the brain with violet light using creative visualization tools and intention. Also to smile to the brain every day and by stimulating the production of amrita and pinoline which are substances produced by the master glands in the brain. Higher brain activities are also activated via our daily lifestyle and how we spend our time which affects our general field of resonance.

Q: What and where are these master glands in the brain?

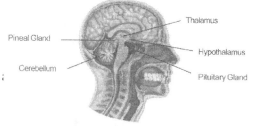

A: These are the pituitary and the pineal glands. They are located in the center of the head. See diagram opposite >

Q: How does a person stimulate these master glands in their brain?

A: Firstly by acting as if these glands are conscious of every thought and word and providing them with specific behavioral commands that are in alignment with their original and natural capacities. E.g. to originally produce only life supporting hormones for longevity. For most people these glands have – over time – begun to produce the death hormone to mirror our belief that everyone needs to die. Next we need to stimulate them to produce more amrita and pinoline which are natural substances that can permeate the brain to alter brain wave activity. These glands can also be stimulated to produce more DMT and 5-MeO-DMT which also alter brain wave patterns.

Q: How is this done?

A: By using creative visualization both glands can be flooded with violet light and in addition:-

a) **For the pituitary gland** we can place the tongue on the roof of the mouth, and each day move it back until the muscles are stretched enough for the tongue to reach up behind the uvula. This must be done with the mindset that the tongue position is stimulating the energy channels that connect from the roof of the mouth directly to the pituitary and that with this stimulation the pituitary gland will increase its natural production of amrita.

b) **For the pineal gland** we can contract and release the muscles around the clitorus in women and the scrotum in men. There is a direct energy channel linking these areas with the pineal gland and as we contract and release the muscles around these sexual centers the pineal gland also contracts and pulses and releases more pinoline which then floods through the brain to feed it so that it then feeds the body in a different way.

Q: Exactly what sort of mental attitudes and mindsets do people need to adopt to successfully experience the benefits of The Prana Program?

A: For successful pranic nourishment an attitude that:-

- ♥ "All my nourishment, all my vitamins, all my minerals, everything I need to maintain a healthy body, comes from prana" is step one.
- ♥ Next an attitude that "I only eat for pleasure, not for need as prana provides all I require" is another new mindset.
- ♥ Both commands help to rewire the brain's neural pathways.
- ♥ Positive thinking increases lifespan.

- ♥ We can also stimulate the master glands and
- ♥ change brain wave patterns via
- ♥ will, intention, creative visualization

and also

- ♥ through meditation and daily lifestyle

THE PRANA PROGRAM
Enjoyable & Effective Evolution with Jasmuheen
e-book at http://www.selfempowermentacademy.com.au/htm/cia-education.asp#pranaprogram

FULL DETAILS ON:

Prana Program Benefits; Prana & the Bio-system; Prana & The Brain; Prana & Darkroom Technology; Prana & The Heart; Prana & The Cells; Prana & Field Science; Prana & Inter-dimensional Life; Preparation, Physical Changes & Pre-programming; Calibration, Testing & Comfortable Conversions; Social Scenes – Prana & Social Scenes; Prana & Parenting; Prana & Other Family Members – Harmonizing Households; Prana & Eating Disorders; Prana & Sexuality; Global Issues – Gifts & Growth – Past, Present & Future; Prana & Health; Prana & Religion; The Prana Program & the Environment; The Prana Program & Politics; Skeptics & the Media; plus Solar Nourishment, Bigu & The Bigger Picture are in Chapters 2 to 8 of THE PRANA PROGRAM.

- ♥ Certain Mental Attitudes & Mindsets need to be understood & adopted in order to begin to be nourished by prana.
- ♥ Once we understand what prana is, and how it can feed us, then we need to expect it to.
- ♥ Thoughts create reality and chi follows mind.

THE PRANA PROGRAM
Mental Attitudes

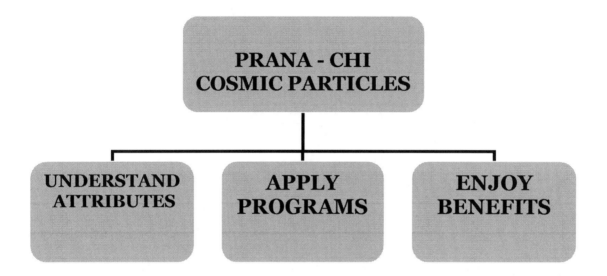

Part B:-
COMMUNITY LIFE – ADULTS INFLUENCING THE FIELDS & CREATING A NOURISHING AND SUPPORTING FIELD FOR THEMSELVES AND THEIR CHILDREN.

Q: How can you expect children under 5 or even older, to be aware of the need to hold certain mental attitudes towards their nourishment? Surely all a small child understands is the ache of hunger in their stomach?

A: A journalist once said to me that young children die each minute from starvation and malnutrition and that changing our beliefs and mindset about nutritional requirements of food would not save them. However when we understand the dynamics of energy, we understand that children are linked to their parents' energy fields, particularly that of the mother, until they are 18 months to 2 years old. They then begin the process of separation, which some schools of thought say is completed between 14 and 21, depending on the individual. Change the lifestyles and beliefs of the parent and the community and the child will change. Hence in The Prana Program we need to educate experientially the adults first who can then hold the field of support for the children.

There is a wonderful story that I once heard that demonstrates the 'creating and holding a nourishing field idea'. Years ago when I was researching the Bigu phenomena in the Qigong communities I was told of a family in New York where neither the parents, nor the children, nor the goldfish, and not even the pot plants needed any food. Apparently the field emanation of love from the parents was so strong that everything within their field was fed pranically and needed no physical food as nourishment.

Many of us have found that people who are continually exposed to our presence begin to be fed in other ways and eventually naturally their hungers subsided.

Q: What research statistics can you share that may inspire this change.

A: The facts are that malnutrition contributes to nearly seven million child deaths every year – more than any infectious disease, war or natural disaster, according to the *1998 State of the World's Children Report* released by UNICEF, the United Nations Children's Fund.

No less than half of all children under the age of five in South Asia and one-third of those in sub-Saharan Africa, as well as millions of children in industrialized countries, are malnourished. Three-quarters of the children who die worldwide of causes related to malnutrition are what nutritionists describe as "mildly to moderately malnourished" and show no outward signs of problems. Consciously adding prana as an additional nutrition source can only be beneficial especially when we consider:-

- ☹ The approximate number of children who starve to death every day: 40,000
- ☹ How frequently a child dies of starvation: Every 2 seconds
- ☹ The number of people who will starve to death each year: >60 million
- ☹ The number of pure vegetarians who can be fed on the amount of land needed to feed 1 person consuming a meat-based diet: 20. (This number could be closer to 150 if you're talking about pure rawfood-vegetarians.)
- ☺ The number of people who could be adequately fed by the grain saved if Americans reduced their intake of meat by 10%: 60 million.
- ☺ Number of people who can be nourished by prana: limitless
- ☺ $ cost of pranic nourishment and production = $0

Q: How do you hope to address the challenge of educating adults in these communities and inspiring them to adopt the prana mindset?

A: When adults are exposed to the reality of many individuals worldwide being able to live on prana, they will lose their fear and change their mindset. This will lead to a modification in the frequency and quality of the energy they emit, and their children will respond accordingly. Everything is interconnected. The secret is in the understanding of the power of the mind over our molecular structure and although those who have not felt the power of their DOW may not understand the experience of feeling interconnected to everything, nonetheless education with practical tools will help.

It is also important to keep our focus clear. The pranic nourishment solution is a bridge to freedom only because it is one way to unlock the majestic power of our DOW. It is not about whether we eat or don't eat, but whether we need to. It is about being free from the erroneous fear that says, "If we don't eat food we will die", and it is also a wonderful skill to have in times of famine from war or Earth changes. This is part of the new mindset that needs to be offered into communities that are dependant on external food resources in a way that is detrimental to them.

Q: What do you mean by 'dependant on external food resources in a way that is detrimental to them'?

A: If food resources are being sent to these countries but they are not being appropriately distributed – as has been the case with some of the African aid – then it is imperative that the local population are taught to unhook themselves from their dependancy on the performance of others and in this way education into The Prana Program can help as it promotes self reliance.

An Indian guru I knew once said: "Never be dependant on anything outside of yourself" and now that we have experientially researched prana's nutritonal aspects then we can offer this also as an aid. Providing tools and education to move beyond victim consciousness is a very beneficial evolutionary program.

Q: You touched on this in Chapter 7 but can you share more regarding how The Prana Program will combat world hunger issues, particularly re resource redistribution?

A: The success of pranic nourishment in combating global hunger is dependant on a massive re-education program into self-responsibility and self-refinement that honors all our bodies from the physical to the spiritual.

How long until eating for pleasure rather than for need becomes an everyday possibility in the west, is up to each one of us, and as more of us allow our DOW to sustain us, then the sooner the idea of not needing to eat food can move from the miraculous into the everyday and into Third World countries.

It is actually the 8 point Luscious Lifestyle Program that if adopted by more, will bring the most dramatic change. When this lifestyle is applied in the west many people will naturally become more service-minded and more active in compassionately addressing the problems of others. So much can be taught freely to change what is happening in Third World situations by the re-education of all. As we find our emotional and mental nourishment moving from beyond greed for material things, we can effectively redistribute needed resources.

Q: You stress the need for holistic education, so exactly what do you feel needs to be taught in countries with hunger and lack of nutrition challenges?
A: Firstly as all people can breathe and breathing is free, this is the first tool to teach people regardless of where they now live. To do pranayama, means to do particular breathing exercises that feed and nourish the energy fields of all the human bodies.

Pranayama breathing exercises and even qigong can easily be taught to young and old to improve their health and vitality levels. Coupled with programming and mind power techniques, radical transformations can be made regardless of our circumstances. All can use the breath techniques in Part C daily and feel the difference.

More can also be immediately taught about the amazing capabilities of the human bio-system including the mind/body connection, and how to effectively reprogram ourself to be free from limiting beliefs. We need to understand mentally how prana is a viable alternative source of nourishment that is available now and for free.

People die from starvation because they have not yet been taught about this alternative nutrition source, or about mind mastery and the power of their focused thought to create a different reality. Many have not yet discovered the true power of the Divine Force within and how breath techniques can nourish them on all levels as they are too busy trying to survive. Being able to live without food from the physical realms becomes quite simple when we understand how and it will make the survival game easier for many.

To reiterate: Breathing is free and breath techniques can be taught to gain increased nourishment and health and longevity. Thinking is free, so mind mastery programming techniques can also be taught immediately. The power of prayer and healing through song can be taught as well as a basic understanding of universal law. It all just needs to be delivered in an easy to understand conceptual framework with simple pragmatic tools.

Q: You often talk about reducing the expenditure on weaponry, can you discuss this more?

A: Definitely, before the war on terrorism, the World Bank released statistics that showed that just one third of our annual global military budget could be redirected each year to eliminate global poverty. We also know that warfare has been the most common human cause of famine for in addition to destroying crops and food supplies, warfare also disrupts the distribution of food through the use of siege and blockade tactics.

Our proposal for eventual global disarmament will eliminate this problem of warfare and many of us are now in service pragmatically creating change for global civility. With pranic nourishment we do not need to grow crops, so famine from drought will not be a problem. With pranic nourishment we do not need to slaughter animals or even eat a 'balanced diet' and we will not get malnutrition, as all that our body needs can come from prana when we learn how.

Simplistically our global expenditure on weaponry is because we live in fear; and increasing the pranic flow eliminates fear and makes us more compassionate so we have no need for such destructive weaponry.

THE PRANA PROGRAM
Enjoyable & Effective Evolution with Jasmuheen
e-book at http://www.selfempowermentacademy.com.au/htm/cia-education.asp#pranaprogram

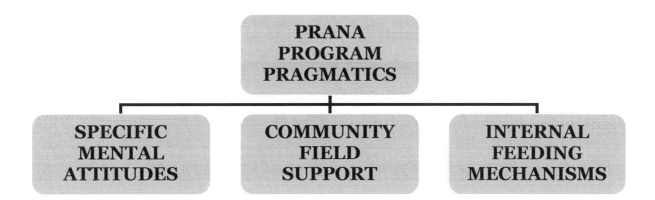

Part C:-
ALTERNATE PRAGMATIC INTERNAL FEEDING MECHANISMS
Plus Breathing Rhythms

Breathing rhythms: We know that one way that prana comes in is via our breath. In fact some say that we receive 70% of our nourishment independent of food via breathing. Prana is an invisible force field that permeates every atom and we can manufacture more of it throughout our body at will. Meditation on our breath can increase the flow and potency of prana through our cells. We can practice deep breathing exercises and imagine that with every breath we are filling our lungs and cells with a powerful dosage of nutrients that are contained within the invisible prana.

There are numerous breath techniques to draw more prana into the body that people of all countries and cultures can freely utilize. When we squint our eyes we can see prana sparkling in the air. Prana is everywhere, and as we mentioned earlier, some sources say that the majority of our nutritional needs can be fulfilled by the way we breathe.

Pranayama involves controlling the breath which in turns controls the effectiveness of many of the functions of the body. Long slow breaths slow the heart, deep breathing warms us; oxygen eliminates pain, slow breathing promotes health and longevity.

In the Encyclopaedia Britannica, it is written: "Sanskrit PRANA ("breath"), in Indian philosophy, the body's vital "airs", or energies. A central conception in early Hindu philosophy, particularly as expressed in the Upanishads, prana was held to be the principle of vitality and was thought to survive as a person's "last breath" for eternity or until a future life".

Breathing Techniques for magnetizing and increasing the pranic flow using the love breath meditation and the Ancient Vedic Holy Breath tool. Both of the following techniques increase the amount of nourishing chi and prana in the body and expand our cells capacity to attract and radiate nutrition from the Theta-Delta field. We then add additional techniques such as pranayama and basic pranic breathing.

Our breath is one of the most powerful tools we have for the feeding and fine tuning of our bio-system. Free, and at our constant control, we can utilize various breath techniques to achieve many things from calming and de-stressing the bio-system to increasing the pranic flow and improving our health and more. While there are many techniques of breath work, for the Divine Nutrition – Prana Program, I recommend the below two.

Breath Technique no. 1:

This technique is designed to tune us to attract a different mix of cosmic particles. I call it the **Love Breath meditation**. Do for at least 5-10 minutes each morning and evening or until you really feel as if all you are is love and all you do comes from this love. Do the following 3 steps every morning and as much as you remember to do it and see how you feel after a month or so …

- Step 1 – imagine yourself connected on the inner planes with a beam of pure love that flows from the heart of the Divine Mother* into your heart chakra.
- Step 2 – Inhale of this love deeply and chant as you inhale "I am love". Keep chanting this mantra over and over with sincerity and know that the chant is opening all your fields to love.
- Step 3 – Exhale this love slowly out into your body and chant "I love" over and over with sincerity as you imagine this love filling every cell and then flowing out from your auric field and into your outer world.
- Also with this tell your body over and over until it tingles "I love you, I love you, I love you, I love you" as per technique no. 3.

(* or a never ending source of pure love.)

This exercise opens our cells to receiving pure Divine Mother Love as it strengthens our Divine heart and our ability to attract, hold and radiate love in this world. It also helps to change our brain wave patterns from Beta-Alpha to the Theta-Delta zone.

This is definitely a 'try it and experience the difference' tool which takes some focus and discipline. As we have shared in other manuals, a basic breathing technique like this one which uses the "I am love, I love" mantra, is also a wonderful way to train what the Indian yogis call our 'monkey' mind to remain still and focused. Many western people are unable to focus their mind on just their breath for more than a minute or two without finding themselves thinking of work, or shopping, or other things, yet mind mastery is absolutely necessary to enjoy the full benefits of The Prana Program. Untrained in the art of stillness, the western mind in particular requires this type of training as a pre-requisite for attaining inner and outer peace.

Technique no. 2:

The Ancient Vedic Holy Breath. Over 5000 years old this technique achieves a number of things. Firstly what actually breathes us is our DOW – the Divine One Within us who is here to have a human experience and who utilizes our physical, emotional and mental bodies to do so. Without Its energy we could not and would not exist and when we match Its breathing rhythm we begin to glimpse Its power of nourishment. Using this tool is also like saying to your DOW "Are you there? I really want to experience you".

- ☺ Take a few moments and sit in stillness then,
- ☺ Breathe through your nose with deep, fine and connected breaths, no pausing as you inhale then exhale so that you are literally circular breathing.
- ☺ Once you have an even rhythm, move your awareness to the energy behind your breath and just watch and feel your breathing rhythm.
- ☺ Remember you are focusing now on the inner force that breathes you and you will know when you have found Its rhythm as you will begin to feel Its waves of love pulsating through you.
- ☺ After awhile you will no longer be focused on deep, fine connected breathing and instead will feel as if you are being breathed.

Technique no. 3:

Pranic Breathing: Master Choa Kok Sui, founder of the pranic healing movement says pranic breathing is done by:

- ☺ Connecting your tongue to your palate.
- ☺ Doing abdominal breathing *(through the nostrils)*.
- ☺ Inhaling slowly and retain for one count.
- ☺ Exhaling slowly and retain for one count before exhaling which is called 'empty retention.'
- ☺ You can also inhale for 7 counts and retain for one count then exhale for 7 counts and retain for one count, or do 6 and retain for 3.

"In doing abdominal breathing, you expand your abdomen slightly when inhaling and contract your abdomen slightly when exhaling. Do not over-expand or over-contract your abdomen."

THE PRANA PROGRAM
Enjoyable & Effective Evolution with Jasmuheen
e-book at http://www.selfempowermentacademy.com.au/htm/cia-education.asp#pranaprogram

---

The following is an excerpt from his book *Miracles through Pranic Healing*.

"Prana or ki is that life energy which keeps the body alive and healthy. In Greek it is called *pnuema*, in Polynesian *mana*, and in Hebrew *ruah*, which means "breath of life" …

"Basically, there are three major sources of prana: Solar prana, air prana, and ground prana. Solar prana is prana from sunlight. It invigorates the whole body and promotes good health. It can be obtained by sunbathing or exposure to sunlight for about five to ten minutes and by drinking water that has been exposed to sunlight. Prolonged exposure or too much solar prana would harm the whole physical body since it is quite potent.

"Prana contained in the air is called air prana or air vitality globule. Air prana is absorbed by the lungs through breathing and is also absorbed directly by the energy centers of the bioplasmic body. These energy centers are called chakras. More air prana can be absorbed by deep slow rhythmic breathing than by short shallow breathing. It can be also absorbed through the pores of the skin by persons who have undergone certain training.

"Prana contained in the ground is called ground prana or ground vitality globule. This is absorbed through the soles of the feet. This is done automatically and unconsciously. Walking barefoot increases the amount of ground prana absorbed by the body. One can consciously draw in more ground prana to increase one's vitality, capacity to do more work, and ability to think more clearly.

"Water absorbs prana from sunlight, air, and ground that it comes in contact with. Plants and trees absorb prana from sunlight, air, water, and ground. Men and animals obtain prana from sunlight, air, ground, water, and food. Fresh food contains more prana than preserved food."

Technique no. 4:

Pranayama from: http://www.lavecchia.com/pranayama2.html

Note: Pranayama training demands mastery over the asanas (yoga postures) and the strength and discipline arising from them.

- ☺ Before starting pranayama the bowels should be evacuated and the bladder emptied.
- ☺ Preferably pranayama should be practiced on an empty stomach.
- ☺ Light food may be taken half an hour after finishing.
- ☺ The best time for practicing is in the early morning before sunrise and after sunset. According to the *Yoga Pradipika*, pranayama should be practiced four times a day, in the early morning, noon, evening and midnight.

Ujjayi Pranayama (victory breath)

- ☺ Sit in any comfortable position.

- ☺ Keep back erect and equal pressure on the seat bones.
- ☺ Stretch the arms out and rest the back of the wrists on the knees.
- ☺ Join index finger and tips of the thumbs. (This is known as *Jnana Mudra*, the symbol of knowledge. The index finger represents the individual soul and the thumb the Universal Soul, union = knowledge.)
- ☺ Close the eyes and look inwards.
- ☺ Exhale completely.
- ☺ Take a slow, deep steady breath through both nostrils. The passage of the incoming air is felt on the roof of the palate and makes a sound (saaa). This sound should be heard.
- ☺ Fill the lungs up, be careful not to bloat the abdomen in the process of inhalation.
- ☺ The entire abdominal area from the pelvic wall up to the sternum should be pulled back towards the spine.
- ☺ Hold the breath for a second or two.
- ☺ Exhale slowly, deeply and steadily, until the lungs are completely empty. Keep the abdomen tight for a few seconds, relax the diaphragm slowly. The outgoing air should brush the upper palate making a (ha).
- ☺ Wait a moment before drawing in another breath.
- ☺ Repeat the cycles for 5-10 minutes keeping the eyes closed.
- ☺ Lie on the floor in *Savasana* (corpse pose).

Effects

This type of Pranayama opens the lungs, removes phlegm, gives endurance, soothes the nerves and tones the system. Ujjayi without the retention of the breath and reclining position of the body is ideal for people with high blood pressure or coronary troubles. *Be sure to consult your acting physician.*

Pranayama – Breath Technique with David Wolfe

From his book *The Sunfood Diet Success System* page 316, David writes, "First and foremost, the breath controls the energy level in the body. We know that everything is energy – matter is just a form of frozen energy. The more oxygen available to your cells, the more energy you have to accomplish your goals and the less food you desire. Many people overeat because they are not breathing properly.

"If you feel hungry, sick, tired or worn out, a good way for you to quickly rejuvenate yourself is to go outside and take 30 deep diaphragmatic breaths ... In my opinion, the best pattern for deep diaphragmatic breathing, which I have used daily since age 19, is the following 1:4:2: ratio:

- ☺ **Breathe in** (through the nose), for a multiple of 1 count. The nose simultaneously filters and humidifies the air we breathe. The cribriform plate above the septum in the nose also regulates the temperature of the air entering the lungs.
- ☺ **Hold that breath** for a multiple of 4 counts. This fully oxygenates and stimulates the body.
- ☺ **Breathe out** (through the mouth), for a multiple of 2 counts. The outbreath releases toxins.
- ☺ An example of this ratio: Breathe in for 6 seconds; hold that breath for 24 seconds; breathe out for 12 seconds.

Also try this yogic breath technique:

- ☺ **Breathe in** (through the nose), for a multiple of 1 count.
- ☺ **Hold that breath** for a multiple of 1 count.
- ☺ **Breathe out** (through the mouth), for a multiple of 1 count.
- ☺ **Hold the lungs empty** for a multiple of 1 count. This creates a vacuum suction which draws toxins out of the tissues on the following inhalation.
- ☺ An example of this ratio: Breathe in for 6 seconds; hold that breath for 6 seconds; breathe out for 6 seconds. Hold lungs empty for 6 seconds.

'Breath power' is well known in meditation circles, as I wrote in my book *In Resonance* in the chapter called "The Breath of Life": "It has been said that if we were to change nothing – not our eating, exercise or thinking patterns and habits – except our breathing pattern, we could radically alter our life span ... if we reduce the number of breaths that we breathe per minute from say fifteen to five, we will triple our lifespan ...

"Apart from aiding in maintaining and restoring health and vitality and increasing longevity, the main benefit of seeking to experience the 'breath of life' (the energy that sustains us) is that, due to Its very pure and perfect nature, when we contact and experience It, we are given a range of experiences from deep inner peace, total complete relaxation and better sleep, to the overwhelming feelings of joy and bliss of nirvana or Samadhi."

As Choa Kok Sui says, "We get most of our ki or life energy from the air we breathe ... We constantly drain our life energy or ki by our every thought, every act of will or motion of muscles. In consequence replenishment is necessary, which is possible through breathing and other helpful practices".

THE PRANA PROGRAM
Enjoyable & Effective Evolution with Jasmuheen
e-book at http://www.selfempowermentacademy.com.au/htm/cia-education.asp#pranaprogram

MIND POWER AND BREATHING RHYTHMS

Before we proceed to offer simple internal feeding meditation mechanisms it is important to use all of the breathing techniques with the intention that all our vitamins, minerals and nutrients come to us via prana which we are absorbing through breath in the ways discussed. This mental focus adds more power to the practice.

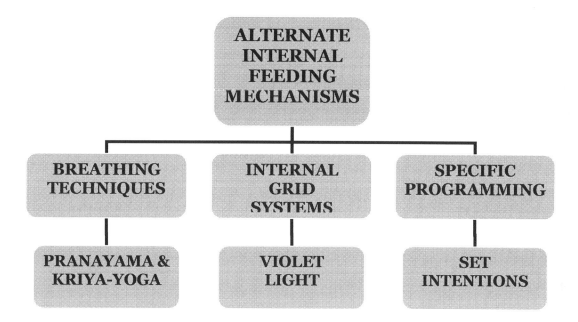

INTERNAL FEEDING SYSTEMS

While we offer some more complex internal feeding and hydration systems in my books *The Food of Gods* and *The Law of Love*, I believe that the below is sufficient to begin our prana program within Third World countries. The meditations and visualization processes are simple enough and will be very effective when used with mind power, will and intention, plus an understanding of pranic attributes which will also need to be taught.

Pranic System Flush and hydration with breath rhythm:

A tool that uses Creative Visualization, programming and breath for nourishing and hydrating the body – this is for those who wish to know how to nourish and hydrate their systems using a more metaphysical method.

☺ Sit or lie down comfortably, center yourself and begin the love breath meditation.

☺ Inhale deeply from the never ending well of Divine Love in your heart and chant: "I am love" and then exhale and chant "I love". This is your cosmic particle door opener that puts you automatically in touch with all the love in all the fields from which true nourishment comes.

☺ Tell the body over and over "I love you, I love you, I love you" – this prepares the cells receptivity levels to absorb and receive more love and cosmic particles and also expands their capacity to hold them.

☺ Next visualize that your feet are resting in a beautiful cool, bubbling glade of highly energized chi water that is sparkling with golden violet hues of pure nourishing energy. Imagine that this is a magical pool offered to you by Mother Earth.

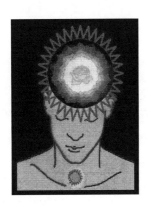

☺ Next move your mind up to your crown chakra and imagine that all of the thousand petals of the lotus that sits in this chakra are open and that a thousand beams of violet light are radiating from each petal, searching out in a 360 degree direction to connect with and magnetize all the cosmic particles of pure chi energy that you need.

☺ Imagine these beams also now anchoring themselves into a vast, nourishing cool blue universal ocean – an ocean of pure hydrating and nourishing chi.

☺ Now establish a breathing rhythm where each inhale is connected with each exhale, breathe deep, fine and connected circular breathing.

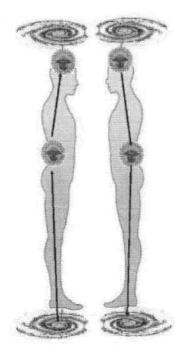

☺ As you breathe in deeply, imagine that you are now drawing in through the soles of your feet, all the nourishing and hydrating liquid that your body needs, draw it from this pool, draw it up through your feet, through your ankles, through your calves, through your bones, through your muscular structure and blood lines and lymphatic system, draw this cooling liquid right up your legs, through the kidneys and your torso and through to the top of your head.

☺ Imagining as your mind follows your breath, and you draw it up through your body, that you are flooding your whole system with cool energizing chi filled water that comes from the heart of Mother Earth.

- ☺ Then as you breathe out imagine that as you push your breath gently downwards that you are drawing all the universal water through the beams that are anchored in the lotus in your crown chakra and that
- ☺ you are now sending, directing this universal liquid down through your system.
- ☺ Imagine that it flows through your brain hydrating and nourishing it with this magical cosmic particle violet and blue light liquid,
- ☺ imagine sending it down your throat, into your lungs, filling your lungs and then your heart with nourishing liquid from the universal ocean of pure cosmic particles,
- ☺ imagine it then being pushed gently with your exhale down into your kidneys and intestines, through your sexual organs, then down your legs and into your feet and send these universal streams of liquid light back into the pool.
- ☺ Imagine that as you inhale and exhale that you are literally flushing out your whole system, bringing in the water element of Earth from the pool at your feet as you inhale, and then as you exhale you begin to flush out your system as streams of cosmic particles from the universal ocean of chi now flow in through your crown chakra down into your system like an internal shower.
- ☺ Imagine then as you take a deep inhale that you are again drawing more of this perfect hydrating fluid from the pool of water at your feet and again as you exhale you draw it down or in through the crown from the universal ocean to hydrate and nourish you perfectly.
- ☺ Keep repeating this breathing rhythm and holding the visual images in your mind's eye, imagine marrying the waters of the cosmos with the waters of the pool.
- ☺ Imagine that as these streams flow through your body with your inhale and your exhale that your body is being re-energized, nourished and re-hydrated exactly as it needs.
- ☺ Repeat until you intuitively feel that your body has had enough – but do for 5 minutes minimum.

Additional Inner Plane Feeding Codes & Meditation:

The following simple meditation and programming codes are an aid to feed the body from the inner planes. It is a variation on and the next level for, the spinning chakra column meditation in *The Food of Gods* and includes programming with the seven elements. The success of this technique depends totally on your mind/body connection and the belief that you are the Master of this vehicle and that **chi follows mind** and that the body can do anything that it is instructed to do.

Note: This is a feeding mechanism – do before a meal NOT after. Also I find drinking a glass of water before you begin aids the body in handling the electromagnetic boost it is about to receive.

- ☺ Lie or sit in a comfortable position.
- ☺ Use the love breath tool and body love tool so that the body co-operates more easily with us.
- ☺ When you have established a good breathing rhythm then if you feel murmurings in the stomach, ask the body if it is hungry. If you get a 'yes' apply the next step. If you get a 'no' then ask why you are having the murmurings and 'is it due to blocked energy?' If you do get a 'yes' and are still taking nourishment from physical food then you may wish to replace your normal feeding methods for just one meal a day by using the cosmic particles program below.
- ☺ If you get a 'yes' then instruct: "Cells of my body, molecules of my body, I instruct that you draw all that you need to feed and hydrate you now from cosmic particles!"
- ☺ Next continue your instruction with a command said with intention as if you are the master and the body must obey you.
- ☺ Command: "Body feed your self from the Cosmic Fire elements now, body feed from the element Akasha now, body feed from the astral light element now, body feed from the cosmic particles now. Body feed off the elements of air, Earth, fire and water now. Body take all that you need – your vitamins and minerals for your perfect nourishment and hydration – take all this from the universal elements now!"
- ☺ Continue with the chant: "I am fed by cosmic fire now! I am fed by akasha now! I am fed by astral light now! I am fed by the element air now! I am fed by the element fire now! I am fed by the element Earth now! I am fed by the element water now!"
- ☺ Next imagine all the filaments from within all your cells dancing and being revitalized as the violet light attracts all of this from the elements and brings it back into your system to feed it now.
- ☺ Imagine it nourishing and hydrating your light-body, your meridians, your skeleton, your bone marrow, your bloodlines, your organs, your muscles, your nervous system, your lymphatic and endocrine systems and your skin now.

The above meditation can be used in conjunction with the other inner plane feeding tools discussed in *The Food of Gods* particularly the spinning chakra column and feeding through the atoms system which I have personally used with great success.

Additional mindset programs to use may be:
- ☺ "All my nourishment, all my food, all my fluid comes to me from the violet light and the cosmic ocean now!"
- ☺ "All my nourishment, all my vitamins, all my food, all my fluid comes to me via the inner planes from cosmic particles now!"

Use your intuition to find your own mantras but remember that your words must be accompanied by the feeling, the knowing that chi follows mind and that chi has the power to create and sustain all life. Again do this for as long as you are guided and then ask your body if it is still hungry or if it is happy and full. You should feel a shift in your stomach and those flutterings should have abated. It takes approximately 3 days for the stomach to shrink when one stops eating regularly and / or minimizes their food intake.

THE PRANA PROGRAM
Enjoyable & Effective Evolution with Jasmuheen
e-book at http://www.selfempowermentacademy.com.au/htm/cia-education.asp#pranaprogram

COSMIC PARTICLE
FEEDING & HYDRATION
Synopsis

To the left, visual examples of drawing energy from the universal forces using
- ♥ will,
- ♥ intention and
- ♥ visualization.

- ♥ On the inhale draw cool, hydrating, prana from an imaginary pool at our feet.
- ♥ Draw it up through the body, flushing through the kidneys and up to the crown,
- ♥ then ...
- ♥ On the exhale draw the cosmic particles down through crown chakra from universal ocean
- ♥ and send through body,
- ♥ through kidneys,
- ♥ down legs,
- ♥ out through feet chakras and
- ♥ into the inner plane pool at our feet.

- ♥ Inhale and draw energy up,
- ♥ then exhale and
- ♥ send nourishing energy down,
- ♥ all the while imagining cosmic particle energy
- ♥ nourishing and also
- ♥ hydrating the body perfectly.

- ♥ Repeat breathing rhythm for at least 5 minutes every morning.

THE PRANA PROGRAM
Enjoyable & Effective Evolution with Jasmuheen
e-book at http://www.selfempowermentacademy.com.au/htm/cia-education.asp#pranaprogram

Part D:-

SOLAR FEEDING PROGRAM – Micro Food and Research

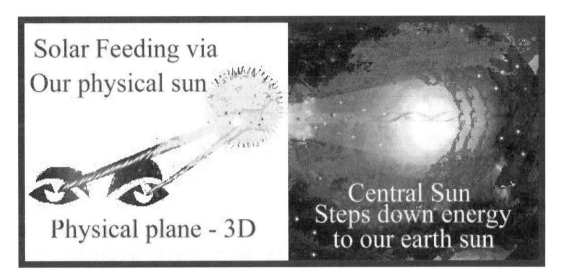

Q: What is solar nourishment?

A: Solar nourishment is an ancient practice of absorbing micro food from the sun through the eyes and pores of our skin, to feed our brain and body.

Q: Who is HRM and what is micro food?

A: HRM is Hira Ratan Manek, a leading proponent and researcher in the field of solar nourishment. In an interview with me in 2002 he said: "I was able to revive an age old practice of sun gazing or SURYANAMASKAR or the present HRM phenomena. As a matter of fact entire humanity was on sun food (micro food) at the beginning and slowly we changed over to a secondary source of food (plants). But at all times in human history many have lived on sun energy and many are also living now and are living for a period much more than me but I am unique only to the extent that I volunteered before medical science for round-the-clock supervision and observations. I have no claim that I have found out how to live on sun energy because it was already there but it had been forgotten and I have only revived it and proved it before science."

Q: What testing has been done with HRM?

A: An International team of 21 Doctors supervised HRM in Ahmedabad for 411 days. He remained only on a diet of water. There were volunteers that were on round-the-clock supervision. Although sun energy is ample for HRM's energy requirements he takes coffee, tea or buttermilk to satisfy his family and doctors.

After the excitement of the findings at Ahmedabad, HRM was invited to Thomas Jefferson University and State University of Pennsylvania in Philadelphia. They wanted to observe and examine his retina, pineal gland and brain. Some of the initial results are that the gray cells in HRM's brain are regenerating. 700 photographs have been taken. Neurons are reported to be active and not dying. The pineal gland is not shrinking which is typically what happens after mid fifties and its maximum average size is about 6 x 6 mm. But for HRM it's been measured to be at 8 x 11 mm.

Q: What type of program does HRM recommend when using the sun for alternate nourishment?
A: According to research provided by Hira Ratan Manek, we begin the program with sun gazing practice for a few minutes at sunrise and sunset, slowly building up our exposure over a nine month period.

He says that: "In 6-months time we are staring to eat the original form of micro food – Our Sun. … as we consume the Original form, the sun, hunger goes down. Then hunger starts to disappear. By eight month you should see hunger almost gone. 9 months or 44 minutes for a dull or weak student or with no belief. Max. 9 months or 44 minutes. Your hunger disappears forever. All mechanisms associated with hunger like aroma, cravings, and hunger pangs disappear. No appetite for food. Energy levels are at a higher level. There is a judgment (having had this experience) that the brain is well activated with the sun energy. We become a solar cooker."

At nine months he says: "We have to give up sun gazing now. Solar science prohibits further gazing after 9 months or 44 minutes for the sake of eye care. The body will get discharged when we stop sun gazing. So we have to recharge. The charge will last for only 6 days. Now we have to start walking on bare foot on bare Earth for 45 minutes daily. Relaxed walking only. No need to walk briskly, jog or run. Any convenient time of the day preferably when the Earth is warmer and sunlight is falling on your body.

"When you walk bare foot an important gland in the brain's center called the pineal gland or the third eye is activated. The big toe of the foot represents this gland. 25 years ago it was considered a useless gland. Now it has become an important gland for study and about 18,000 papers have been published in the recent times. It has always been known as the Seat of the soul. The Pineal gland has optic nerve endings.

"The remaining four toes represent glands too – pituitary, hypothalamus, thalamus and amygdala. Amygdala for the last 2 years has been gaining importance in medical research. It's a nucleus of the sun energy or cosmic energy and plays the important part of photosynthesis via the sunlight reaching the brain through the eye. When you walk bare foot, your body weight stimulates all these 5 glands through your toes. This is strengthened by the Earth heat/energy and the sun prana falling on the head or the crown chakra. The chakras are not in the spinal cord that is an imaginary location; they are definitely in the brain. All these create a magnetic field and the body/brain recharges with the energy of the sun entering in you.

"Relax. Walk 45 minutes for one year and food continues to be without you. After one year of recharging, if you are satisfied with your progress you can give up barefoot walking. Then a few minutes of sun energy falling on you once in 3-4 days is enough. But if you want the immune system to be strengthened then keep on the bare foot walking. Also if you want memory power or intelligence to increase please continue the walking practice. As you increase the sun's heat on your feet the brain will activate more and more. Pineal gland will become more active."

Simple Solar Nourishment Program (modified by Jasmuheen):-
- ♥ Begin gazing directly at sun – dawn and dusk for a few minutes each time, expect prana to provide all your nutrients to maintain health.
- ♥ Slowly build up exposure over a nine month period till you are at 44 minutes maximum solar gazing then stop daily practice.
- ♥ Barefoot walk for 45 minutes each day for one year – to absorb ground and air prana and stimulate acupressure points in the feet to alter your brain wave patterns.
- ♥ Then every 3-4 days do solar gazing as a maintenance program.
- ♥ Live a virtuous life.

HRM recommends these books for the curious: *Light: Medicine of the Future* by Jacob Lieberman; *The Healing Sun: Sunlight and Health in the 21st Century* by Richard Hobday. I recommend that if possible you do barefoot backwards walking preferably on a beach or in an open environment.

ADDITIONAL RESEARCH ON PRANA, BIGU AND HEALING

Q: You say that the qigong community have done a lot of research into Bigu, can you provide more data on this?

Answer with Eltrayan: Yes, on page 286 in the book *Scientific Qigong Exploration* by nuclear physicist Lu Zuyin, he shares further about the state of *Bigu* and also about the experiments conducted on people who have not eaten for up to 6 years. "*Bigu* is a state in which a person maintains a normal life without taking any food. Standard *Bigu* means very little or no intake of water. Basic *Bigu* means only drinking water and juice. Non-standard *Bigu* means ingesting water, juice and occasionally juicy fruits and vegetable soups."

Q: Are there any documented researched cases of Bigu?

Answer with Eltrayan: Yes a Chinese girl in New York has been in a state of 'Bigu' since 21 October 1987 when she attended a prana emitting lecture by a prana master. At that time she was aged 10. After 10 months from the start of her Biju, the Chinese Military Academy of Medicine organised 8 medical experts to conduct a month long investigation of her. They reached the conclusion that in spite of her extremely insufficient intake of calories and nutrition she had maintained her normal life and growth and the stability of internal physiological conditions. A light duty worker normally needs 2,200 kilocalories each day, but her daily nutrition consumption was only 200 to 300 kilocalories each day, and calculations showed that according to her daily activities, that she needed at least 1500 kilocalories per day. These facts seriously challenged modern physiology.

OTHER RESEARCH

In 1998, a journalist called Stephen Janetzko gave me an article that I believe was published in November 1976, by Germany's Esotera Magazine. It contained an in-depth article called "Sei wurden zu menschlichen Pflanzen" (or "They Changed to Human Plants") and it appears to have been written by Von Dr. Albert A. Bartel.

Focusing on the work of Dr Karl Graninger, it also reports on Maria Furtner from Frasdorf in Bavaria who lived 52 years drinking only water from the mineral spring near her home. Maria underwent a three week observation period in Munich University Hospital to prove she didn't need to eat. When released from the hospital she walked the 60km home in three days without problem.

Then there was Resl – Theresa Nuemann, who I mention in my first book. She lived in the Bavarian Forest in Konnersreuth. Her only food each day for 17 years was a consecrated wafer. X-rays showed her bowels to be pencil thin.

Then there was Anna Nassi, who was the child of a farmer from Deutenhofen in Bavaria. Her teacher told the researchers for the article that Anna lived for 6 years on only water.

After the First World War in Europe, Austrian specialist Dr Karl Graninger noticed that although people had become prisoners of war, not all returned from the war camps unhealthy. For some the fasting, fresh air, meagre diets and non-smoking was very beneficial physically.

The idea that some had starved and were quite ill after imprisonment while others were healthier fascinated him. Consequently from 1920 to 1940 when he died, Dr Graninger conducted research into the phenomena of "inedia paradoxa" – or living without food. Finding 23 cases in the west of Europe, his test subjects were mostly women and children who were observed to live without food for both long and short periods of time. ***All subjects were found to have character attributes of patience, devotion and godliness.***

In Summary:

I share the above research in this section to show that:-
   a) People can healthily survive with minimum calorie intake as in Bigu.
   b) People in war torn areas can find inner resources to sustain them regardless of their circumstances although faith and trust cannot be taught as they come naturally to us through the trials of life.

While we have no proven track record as yet at applying The Prana Program into Third World countries, I personally believe that we can achieve success using a combination of:-

- Breath tools including pranic Breathing;
- Solar Nourishment – where applicable;
- Lifestyle tools;
- Mind mastery & re-education re mind power;
- Specific Internal Feeding Mechanisms that access alternate internal nutritional energy.

No doubt the program may need refining as we apply it experientially but the basic keynotes for success are here.

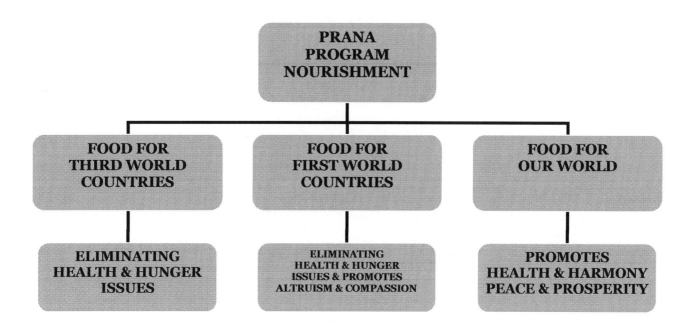

Part E:-

RESOURCE SUSTAINABILITY AND STATISTICS.

The positive impact of The Prana Program on resource sustainability and also on environmental pollution cannot be ignored. These statistics share the difference between a meat based and vegetarian diet. The statistics for the impact of a prana only nourishment are obviously not available but will be far more beneficial again. Regarding health and hunger challenges in Third World countries, research shares that today we have enough resources to feed everyone easily on our planet – we just need more effective distribution systems. However in another few decades even with effective resource distribution systems, we will not have enough resources unless we move to a global vegetarian diet.

Soil

- Historic cause of demise of many great civilizations: Topsoil depletion
- Percentage of original U.S.A. topsoil lost to date: 75%
- Percentage of U.S.A. topsoil loss directly associated with livestock raising: 85%

According to Harvey Diamond a vegetarian lifestyle will save seven hundred million tons of top soil each year and "one hundred and twenty million acres of land, choice land, could be made available for more prudent use".

THE PRANA PROGRAM
Enjoyable & Effective Evolution with Jasmuheen
e-book at http://www.selfempowermentacademy.com.au/htm/cia-education.asp#pranaprogram

Trees

- ☹ Amount of U.S forest which has been cleared to create cropland to produce a meat-centered diet: 260 million acres (1.05 million square kilometres)
- ☹ How often an acre (4,047 square meters) of U.S.A. trees disappears: Every 8 seconds
- ☺ Amount of trees spared per year by each individual who switches to a pure vegetarian diet: 1 acre (4,047 square meters)
- ☺ Amount of tree acreage cleared for prana only nourishment: 0

Rainforests

- ☹ A driving force behind the destruction of the tropical rainforests: American meat habit
- ☹ Current rate of species extinction due to destruction of tropical rainforests and related habitats: 1000 per year.

"The tropical rainforests of the world are probably Earth's most precious resource, offering refuge to three quarters of all living things on the planet. This lush green belt of forest that circles the equator is frequently referred to as Earth's lungs."

Water

- ☺ User of more than half of all water used for all purposes in the United States: Livestock production
- ☺ Water needed to produce 1 pound (.45 kg) of wheat: 25 gallons (95 litres)
- ☺ Water needed to produce 1 pound (.45 kg) of meat: 2,500 gallons (9,465 litres)
- ☺ Water needed to produce prana: 0 gallons
- ☺ Cost of common hamburger meat if water used by meat industry was not subsidized by the U.S.A. taxpayers: $35 per pound ($77 per kg)
- ☺ Current cost for 1 pound (.45 kg) of protein from wheat: $1.50
- ☺ Current cost for 1 pound (.45 kg) of protein from beefsteak: $15.40
- ☺ Cost for 1 pound (.45 kg) of protein from beefsteak if U.S taxpayers ceased subsidizing meat industry's use of water: $89 (Harvey Diamond says the cost is US$35 a pound and that "in California alone the cost of subsidizing the meat industry is US$24 billion per annum!")
- ☺ Current cost for prana protein production: $0

THE PRANA PROGRAM
Enjoyable & Effective Evolution with Jasmuheen
e-book at http://www.selfempowermentacademy.com.au/htm/cia-education.asp#pranaprogram

Petroleum and Energy
- ☹ Length of time world's petroleum reserves would last (with current technologies) if all human beings ate meat-centered diet: 13 years
- ☺ Length of time world's petroleum reserves would last (with current technologies) if all human beings ate vegetarian diet: 260 years
- ☺ Percentage of raw materials consumed in the U.S.A for all purposes presently consumed to produce the current meat-centered diet: 33%
- ☺ Percentage of raw materials consumed in the U.S.A for all purposes needed to produce a pure vegetarian diet: 2%
- ☺ Percentage of raw materials required to produce a pure prana diet: 0%

Sewage Systems
- ☺ Production of excrement by total U.S.A. population: 12,000 lbs. (5443 kg) per second
- ☺ Production of excrement by U.S.A. livestock: 250,000 lbs. (113,400 kg) per second
- ☹ Amount of waste produced annually by U.S.A. livestock in confinement operations which is not recycled: 1 billion tons (907 billion kg)
- ☺ Relative concentration of feedlot wastes compared to raw domestic sewage: Ten to several hundred times more highly concentrated
- ☹ Where feedlot waste typically ends up: Human water supply

Obviously by the above statistics, anyone can see the radical and positive impact that living on prana only will have on our planet in the long term. No need for sewerage systems, no more animal slaughter, no need for such comprehensive systems of waste elimination, no need for such huge oil reserves, and no need for deforestation ... the list goes on.

Part F:-

RESOURCE REDISTRIBUTION AND AID PROGRAMS.

☺ working holistically and harmoniously

☺ combining emotional, mental, spiritual and physical resources

In a recent speech on human rights and peace, the Dalai Lama said:-

"If we are serious in our commitment to the fundamental principles of equality which, I believe, lie at the heart of the concept of human rights, today's economic disparity can no longer be ignored. It is not enough to merely state that all human beings must enjoy equal dignity. This concept must be translated into action. We have a responsibility to find ways to achieve a more equitable distribution of the world's resources.

"We are witnessing a tremendous popular movement for the advancement of human rights and democratic freedom in the world. This movement must become an even more powerful moral force, so that even the most obstructive governments and armies cannot suppress it.

"It is natural and just for nations, peoples and individuals to demand respect for their rights and freedoms and to struggle to end repression, racism, economic exploitation, military occupation, and various forms of colonialism and alien domination. Governments should actively support such demands instead of merely paying lip-service to them."

The Dalai Lama continued: "As we approach the end of the 20th century, we find that the world is becoming one community. We are being drawn together by the grave problems of overpopulation, dwindling natural resources, and an environmental crisis that threaten the very foundation of our existence on this planet. Human rights, environmental protection, greater social and economic equality and peace, are now all interrelated. If we are to meet the challenges of our times, human beings will have to develop a greater sense of universal responsibility.

"We must all learn to work not just for ourselves, our own family or own nation, but for the benefit of all humankind. Universal responsibility is the key to human survival and the best guarantee for human rights and for world peace."

REDIRECTING RESOURCES:

Many people have held concerns for some time about the effects that an ever increasing population growth may have on Earth's future and yet we really have little cause for concern, provided we learn how to effectively redistribute the resources on our planet and take personal responsibility for our lifestyles by working on a holistic level. If we do this then over population should not be a factor of major concern as our resource consumption will be minimized especially as we apply The Prana Program en mass.

Many of us are focused on creating positive personal and planetary progression, not just for ourselves, but also for our offspring and the idea that we can live in harmony and unity as healthy people who respect and honor each other is not just a pipe dream. Yet in order to have healthy, happy and productive adults in society we need to have healthy, happy and productive children.

Q: *How do you suggest that we achieve this?*
A: This is achieved in three ways – home education, school education and life education. Hence it appears that we have a great need for resources to be also redirected into more holistic education programs that provide people with the mental, emotional and even spiritual food required for self mastery, compassion and self reliance, education that promotes compassion, virtues and respect for all life so that resources can be shared more equitably.

NOTE: Chaos upon our planet is not from a lack of goods or services or even the unequal distribution of such. Chaos among humanity comes from a lack of common purpose to unite the diversity of all cultures and societies prevalent today. The chaos we witness on a planetary level comes simply from the:-

- ☹ Lack of honor and tolerance among races and cultures.
- ☹ Lack of clarity on personal and global levels.
- ☹ Lack of vision that we are one people sharing one planet.
- ☹ Lack of purpose and drive in our personal existence.
- ☹ Lack of awareness of why we are truly here and what we can achieve as a species, and
- ☹ Lack of knowledge of the higher nature of our being and of universal laws, which govern the forces of creation.

In the book *Ambassadors of Light* we looked at:-

- ☺ The human resource factor; Education in the new millennium; Tithing and aid organizations; The benefits of the dissolution of prohibition; The benefits of global disarmament; The forgiveness of Third World debt and Raising money for social welfare programs.

So I will not repeat all of this here. What I would like to focus on is what each individual can do immediately independent of governments.

Q: So what do you recommend to an individual regarding minimizing their resource usage? How does The Prana Program help with this?

A: As we utilize more of the pranic stream to nourish us physically, emotionally, mentally and spiritually, we naturally find ourselves consuming less resources. Western civilization consumes many resources to satisfy deep emotional and mental hungers and many find that materialism fails to deliver true satisfaction and yet we continue seeking fulfillment for these hungers.

Metaphysicians and yogi's have long realized that the only source of true nourishment for all our hungers comes from within and when this occurs our lives and consumptions are simplified for we have different drives. The Prana Program and its lifestyle satisfies our deepest hungers thus unhooking us from rampant consumerism, allowing us to live in greater fields of harmony and respect for resources and the needs of others.

MAXIMIZING INTERNAL HUMAN RESOURCES MEANS DECREASING DEPENDANCE ON EXTERNAL GLOBAL RESOURCES = GREATER FREEDOM FOR ALL.

Summary of The Prana Program:
a) Increase internal pranic flow and external prana radiation from our beings and decrease our dependence on the world's resources as we get healthier and need less.
b) Do this via mindest changes, will and intention and the use of alternate internal feeding mechanisms.
c) Promote holistic education programs that allow everyone to be nourished on deeper levels from an alternate source that is free and non-biased.

Outcome: Minimal (if any) health and hunger challenges on Earth.

Q: Is there any final statement that you would like to make to complete the last decade of your research as summarised in this manual?

A: Using the science of the fields to change life, to be more honouring and harmonious for all, to me is basic common sense as it's just utilising our innate abilities more consciously and effectively. We have experientially now had intense and prolonged exposure to the micro-food of life and have begun to understand many of its aspects. We have seen what it can offer to our evolution and how micro-food nourishment can radically improve the quality of human existence. To ignore it, and to deny respect and support for those who research it so that we can share its gifts globally, would greatly lessen both the enjoyment and effectiveness of our evolutionary path. Prana power is a powerful peace, healing and feeding tool for our world and its benefits are destined to be legendary.

For more Positive Planetary Paradigms go to
The Cosmic Internet Academy (C.I.A.) at
www.selfempowermentacademy.com.au

THE PRANA PROGRAM
Enjoyable & Effective Evolution with Jasmuheen
e-book at http://www.selfempowermentacademy.com.au/htm/cia-education.asp#pranaprogram

THE PRANA PROGRAM
GLOBAL CONSCIOUSNESS RE-CALIBRATION FOR CO-CREATING HEALTH & HARMONY

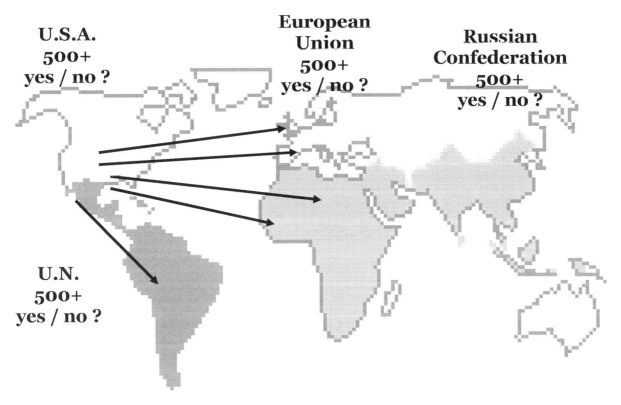

When David Hawkins's book *Power vs. Force* was first published in 1995, his research shared that only 4% of the world's population calibrated at over 500, while in 2004 it is now 6%.
- ☺ A person calibrating at wisdom 300 has the enough DOW power radiation to energetically influence, and even feed by our presence, 90,000 people;
- ☺ at a calibration of 700 we can counterbalance the energy of, and feed, 700 million.
- ☺ Countries must first shift their own calibration to 500, then with this base frequency of love and wisdom they can be influential in global affairs.

**COUNTRY 'CALIBRATION OF CONSCIOUSNESS'
SCALE REQUIRED FOR GLOBAL ADVISORY POSITIONS:
540+ FOR PRESIDENTS; 500+ FOR ANY POLITICIAN OR POLITICAL ADVISOR**
Individual country calibration must be 300+ to provide aid, 500+ to provide advice.
If you can't measure it then you can't manage it. Use sway tool or kinesiology to test.

200 level of truth & integrity; 310 willingness & inspiration; 400 understanding & wisdom; 500 love & revelation; 540 unconditional love, oneness & serenity; 600 peace & illumination & perfection; 700 pure consciousness, DOW merged & in a harmonious state of mastery.

INDEX

A
Acupuncture Points – 49
Abdominal Breathing – 159
Aging Process – 28, 97, 194
Air Prana / air vitality globule – 24, 30, 160, 171
Akasha – 48, 138, 166
Akashic Records – 14, 74, 75
Albert Einstein – 51
Alchemical – 42, 49, 75, 85, 103
Alchemical Initiations – 75
Allopathic and Alternate Testing – 128
Alpha – 15, 32, 41, 42, 96, 148, 158
Alternative Food Source – 24
Amplitude – 41
Amrita – 149, 150
Ancient Wisdoms – 42, 56
Ancient Yogi's – 37, 55
Angelic Realms – 20
Anorexics / Anorexia – 104, 110
Archangels – 41
Arthur Schopenhauer – 127
Aromatherapy – 65
Asanas – 71, 160
Ascension – 17, 18, 40, 56, 115, 117, 123
Ashtanga-Yoga – 63, 71
Astral Light – 48, 138, 166
Atomic Structure – 16
Atoms – 24, 28, 30, 45, 51, 86, 134, 135, 166

B
Beta – 15, 32, 41, 92, 96, 129, 148, 158
Beings of Light – 18, 56
Bhakti-Yoga – 71
Bigger Picture – 28, 85, 110, 134, 139
Bigu – 134, 136-138, 142, 153, 171-173
Biofeedback Looping – 50
Biofield – 49, 50, 103, 117
Biofield Grids – 49, 50
Biological Changes – 30
Bio-electric Currents – 138
Biological Oscillator – 35
Bioplasmic Body – 24, 160
Bio-system – 18, 23, 29, 30, 32-34, 37, 41, 42, 44, 48-50, 52, 58, 60, 65, 66, 68, 76, 80, 82, 91, 98, 103, 124, 155, 158
Bio-shield – 96
Bliss – 42, 43, 71, 78, 162
Blueprints – 21, 50, 68, 74, 102, 103, 128
Body Weight – 60, 71, 81, 89, 170
Brain – 14-16, 21, 28, 32, 35-45, 55, 59, 64, 72, 85, 98, 105, 127, 128, 132, 134, 135, 138, 146, 148-150, 158, 165, 169, 170, 171
Brain Function – 42, 43
Brain Orgasms – 105
Brain Wave Patterns – 15, 16, 37-39, 41, 42, 55, 72, 128, 132, 138, 148, 149, 158, 171

THE PRANA PROGRAM
Enjoyable & Effective Evolution with Jasmuheen
e-book at http://www.selfempowermentacademy.com.au/htm/cia-education.asp#pranaprogram

Breath – 13, 18, 24, 26, 37, 39, 44, 55, 83-85, 93, 96, 145, 147, 155, 157-166, 173
Breatharian – 63, 77, 89, 90, 116, 117
Breath Power – 39, 162
Breathing Techniques – 43, 145, 157, 163
Buddhist – 55, 56, 67
Bulimics / Bulimia – 104

C

Calibrate – 25, 74, 80, 81, 120
Calibration – 39, 51, 57, 60, 61, 69, 72, 77-83, 85, 87, 89-91, 93-95, 101, 114, 115, 120, 121, 123, 124, 130, 131, 135, 138, 147
Celibacy – 105
Cell – 21, 30, 36, 44-47, 58, 61, 133, 158
Cellular Function – 44, 45
Cellular Memory – 61, 74, 88
Cellular Pulsing – 44, 45
Central Sun – 134
Cerebral Cortex – 40
Cerebrum – 138
Chanting – 43, 65, 158
Chakra – 24, 34, 50, 70, 71, 85, 86, 89, 105, 134, 136, 139, 158, 160, 164-166, 171
Chi – Qi, Ki, Prana – 13-18, 20, 21, 23-34, 36-82, 84-94, 96-106, 108-134, 136-142, 144-151, 153-160, 162-165, 167, 171-176, 178-181
Children – 8, 100-102, 104, 106, 112, 152-154, 173, 178
Chinese Scientists – 53
Chinese Military Academy – 172
Christ – 29, 31, 91, 116
Christed Consciousness – 27, 116, 134
Clairaudient – 14, 29
Clairsentient – 14, 29
Clairvoyant – 14, 29
Clear Communication – 83, 103, 104, 107
Clear Inner Guidance – 83
Cognizance – 79
Coherence – 35-37
Comfortable Conversions – 77
Community Support – 145
Compassion – 21, 35, 37, 43, 65, 110, 113, 116, 118, 121, 132, 138, 148, 178
Consciousness – 7, 14, 18, 20, 26-28, 33, 38, 41, 43-45, 47, 48, 50, 52, 55, 57, 64, 78, 79, 81, 84, 85, 87, 88, 90, 98, 99, 110, 112, 116, 118, 121, 128, 130, 134, 137, 138, 140, 147, 154
Cosmic Computer Bank – 69
Cosmic Fire – 48, 60, 138, 166
Cosmic Particles – 14, 20, 26, 28, 34, 39, 41, 47, 48, 60, 61, 65, 69, 71, 74, 82, 83, 85, 87, 89, 90, 93, 101, 116, 125, 134, 147, 148, 158, 164-167
Cosmic Prana – 30
Cosmic Traveling – 41
Cranium Brain – 36
Crystal Children – 101-102
Cult – 67, 117

D

Darkroom Technology – 43
Database – 79
David Hawkins – 68, 77-79, 80-82, 94, 120, 130
Defaecation – 62
Delta – 15, 21, 32, 41, 42, 64, 65, 96, 103, 158
Dependable Discernment Tools – 83, 86
De-programming – 65

Devotion – 71, 91, 116, 173
Devotional Music – 65
Digestive Systems – 30
Dimensional Biofield Science – 49, 50
Dimensional Energy Field Emmanations – 47
Dimethyltryptamine (DMT) – 42, 43, 134, 149
Ding Jing – 137
Divine Consciousness – 43, 45
Divine Essence – 21-23, 38, 75, 82
Divine Love – 20, 27, 34, 38, 41, 48, 52, 57, 60, 71, 92, 108, 117, 123, 134, 164
Divine Mother's Womb – 43
Divine Nutrition – 7, 30, 66, 70-73, 96, 122, 126, 134, 137, 158
Divine Nutrition Trilogy – 7
Divine One Within – also called DOW – 18, 20, 26, 30, 33, 34, 40, 41, 45, 52, 58, 60, 61, 64, 71, 73, 75, 81-84, 92, 94, 95, 97, 98, 102, 103, 117, 118, 124-127, 130, 154, 155, 159
Divine DNA – 52
DNA – 47, 52
DOS (the Divine Order System) – 50
Downloads – 69
DOW – see "Divine One Within"
DOW Power – 45, 81, 92, 103
Dreamtime – 87
Dr George Goodheart – 77
Dr John Diamond – 77, 78
Dr Karl Graninger – 172
Dr Sudhir Shah – 55, 70, 134-136
Dr Yan Xin – 137
E
Earth Prana – 30
Eastern Mysticism – 102
Ecstasy – 22, 42
Effective Evolution – 7, 40
Electrical Circuitry – 49
Electromagnetic Field – 27, 35, 37
Element Mix – 48
Elimination – 17, 59, 63, 66, 176
Elohim – 41
Emotional Dependence – 66, 88
Encodements – 47, 102
Endocrine System – 68, 166
Enjoyable Evolution – 13, 14, 109
Energy Mathematics   135
Energy Transmissions – 50
Enlightenment – 8, 17, 18, 29, 40, 117, 123
Entelechy – 27
Entrainment – 35, 81
Environmental Impact – 109, 126
Environmental Pollution – 110, 174
Esoteric Principles – 7
Esoteric Training – 69
Etheric – 30, 49, 74
Etheric Imprints – 74
Ethical Economics – 118
Evolution – 7, 13-15, 21, 25, 30, 39, 40, 85, 109, 111, 113, 115, 179
Experiential Research – 7, 19, 21, 33, 109, 129, 137, 144
External Prana – 53, 54, 115, 138

Extracellular Fluid – 40

F
Family – 23, 37, 97, 99, 100, 102-104, 107, 122, 124, 126, 153, 169, 177
Family Love – 37
Fasting – 32, 66, 67, 87, 172
Fatima – 67
Field Flow Mastery – 50
Field Irradiation / Radiation – 51, 92, 110
Field Science – 7, 47, 50, 117
Flooding – 17, 38, 42, 46, 51, 98, 164
Forgiveness – 46, 122, 178
Four Body Fitness – 23, 49, 65
Four Dimensional Freedom – 54
Fountain of Youth – 31, 42, 73
Franz Kafka – 22
Freedom – 16, 25, 28, 34, 49, 53-55, 59, 73, 74, 78, 79, 81, 82, 85, 88, 97, 99, 102, 133, 140, 154, 177, 179
Freedom Agenda – 79, 81, 82
Frequency – 13, 16, 35, 37, 41, 45, 46, 50, 51, 57, 62, 65, 70, 77, 89, 92, 97, 154
Frequency Patterns – 50
Full Body Orgasms – 105
Futuristic Science – 55

G
Gamma Rays – 53, 54
Garden of Eden – 41
Genius – 79
Giri Bala – 31, 55, 70
Grace – 16, 19, 20, 31, 34, 41, 57, 73, 75, 93, 103, 115, 123, 126
Grid Structures – 49
Glands – 15, 31, 38, 42, 45, 60, 67, 68, 136, 148, 149, 170, 171
Global Disarmament – 121, 156, 178
Global Resources – 32, 118, 179
Goddess – 57
Ground Prana / Ground Vitality Globule – 24, 128, 160
Guru – 57, 117, 154

H
Harmonious Heart – 34, 36
Harmonious Paradigm – 49
Harmonizing Households – 102
Hatha-Yoga – 71
Health – 8, 13, 17, 19-21, 23-25, 29, 30, 41, 48, 49, 55, 58, 65, 66, 70, 71, 73, 74, 83, 85, 86, 90, 92, 96, 101, 108-114, 118, 120, 121, 124, 126, 128, 130, 135, 136, 139-142, 144-146, 155, 157, 158, 160, 162, 171, 174, 179, 181
Heart Chakra – 34, 85, 105, 158
Heart Orgasms – 105
Hellenistic Mystery – 67
Holiness – 41
Holistic Education – 18, 21, 23, 24, 33, 76, 80, 98, 106, 110, 111, 113, 120, 127, 147, 155, 178, 179
Holy – 20, 41, 56, 57, 67, 96, 157, 159
Holy Ones – 20, 56, 57, 96
Hormic Energy – 27
Hormones – 31, 42, 45, 68, 134, 149
Human Rights – 7, 13, 47, 121, 148, 177
Humility – 65, 129
Hydration – 48, 82, 85, 90, 93, 125, 163, 166, 168

I
Imagination – 47, 136
Immortal – 31, 33, 52, 58, 85, 86

Incorruptible – 34, 83
Indian Yogis – 19, 158
Indigo Children – 102
Influential Decision Makers – 78
Innernet – 76, 111
Inner Universes – 135
Integrity – 66, 78, 81, 82, 89, 120, 129-131
Internet – 76, 109, 141, 144, 180
Inter-dimensional – 20, 24, 28, 39, 41, 49, 52, 55-57, 123, 134
Interconnectedness – 13, 29
Intergration – 39
Internal Circuitry – 30
Internal Classical Music – 45
Internal Feeding Mechanisms – 24, 39, 43, 86, 89, 90, 142, 145, 157, 173, 179
Internal Pranic Flow – 29, 42, 116, 179
Intuition – 20, 21, 23, 34, 36, 38, 58, 60, 72, 83, 87, 146, 148, 167
Intuitive Knowing – 35

J
Jainism – 67

K
Karmic Debts – 46
Karmic Learning – 7, 92, 147, 148
Karmic Ties – 21, 148
Ki – (Chi, Qi, Prana) – See 'Chi'
Kilocalories – 172
Kinesiology – 58, 67, 77, 78, 80, 83, 84, 181
Knowing – 20, 21, 23, 28, 34, 35, 38, 40, 58, 60, 83, 88, 95, 98, 103, 133, 167
Kriya-Yoga – 55, 69, 70, 71, 96, 163
Kundalini Energy – 49

L
Lactating – 100
Language of Light – 49
Laser Beam – 53
Laughter-Yoga – 71
Lent – 67
Lifestyle – 18-20, 23, 30, 39, 41, 42, 49, 52, 55, 57, 65, 69, 72-74, 77, 82, 84, 85, 89-93, 96, 97, 98, 100, 102, 104, 105, 112, 114, 120, 123, 128, 130, 149, 155, 173, 174, 179
Lifestyle Tools – 18, 42, 55, 65, 77, 114, 173
Life Sustaining Hormones – 68
Lightbody – 47, 49, 50, 74
Light Eaters – 30, 92, 98, 100, 132
Light Rays – 49, 50
Linear Thinking – 35
Liquid Crystal Molecules – 115
Live Aid – 122
Livestock Production – 175
Living on Light – 17, 55, 77, 109, 119
Lotus Children – 102
Love Breath Meditation – 157, 158, 163
Lucid Dreaming – 62
Luscious Lifestyle Program – 72, 77, 120, 155

M
Madonna Frequency – 37, 57
Magic – 16, 19, 20, 39
Maharishi – 43
Mahatma Gandhi – 109

Malnutrition – 7, 113, 152, 153, 156
Mana / Manna – 24, 25, 148, 149, 160
Mantak Chia – 35, 43, 105
Mantras – 43, 57, 65, 167
Mantra-Yoga – 71
Master Alchemists – 49
Mathematical Codes – 15, 48
Max Planck – 51
Maximum Potential – 40, 60
Meaning of Life – 47
Media – 11, 32, 76, 81, 108, 109, 123, 127, 129-132, 145
Medication – 64
Meditation – 16, 20, 33, 35, 39, 41, 43, 46, 57, 65, 73, 74, 76, 85, 87, 91-94, 96, 102, 105, 109, 116, 124, 136, 147, 157, 158, 162, 163, 165, 166
Melatonin – 43, 134, 135
Menstruation – 65
Mental Attitudes – 59, 68, 93, 146, 150-152
Meridians – 26, 34, 50, 70, 71, 166
Metabolic Rate – 60, 67, 88
Metaphysical Research – 8
Metaphysician – 15, 18, 23, 46, 65, 117, 179
Metaphysics – 14, 15, 19, 98, 119, 121
Micro Food – 28, 108, 169, 170
Microcosmic Orbit – 70, 105
Mikhael Aivanhov – 70, 140
Mindsets – 42, 58, 59, 145, 146, 150, 151
Mind/Body Connection – 58, 61, 64, 87, 92, 147, 155, 165
Mind Power – 39, 47, 111, 149, 155, 163, 173
Minerals – 32, 45, 59, 64, 150, 163, 166
Minimizing Resource Drainage – 118
Miracles – 19, 34, 102, 160
Modern Physics – 53
Molecules – 16, 30, 43, 115, 166
Morphogenetic Field – 7, 52, 76, 80, 92, 108, 114, 117, 129
Morris Krok – 55
Mortality Patterns – 31, 40, 68, 86
Mother Mary – 57, 67
Motherhood – 100
Multi-dimensional – 29, 33, 55, 60
Muscle Mass – 63, 71
Muslem – 56

N

Niels Bohr – 51
Nervous System – 35, 36, 166
Neural Pathways – 59, 150
Neurohormones DMT & 5-MeO-DMT – 42, 134, 149
Neuronal Activity – 41
Neurons – 35, 40, 170
Neuro-hormones – 134
Neuro-theology – 14, 42
Neutrinos – 53
Newtonian Mechanics – 51
Nutrients – 14, 45, 139, 157, 163, 171
Nutrition – 7, 17, 25, 28, 30, 46, 48, 64, 66, 70-73, 79, 88, 90, 91, 96, 109, 118, 122, 125, 126, 128, 129, 134, 137-139, 144, 147, 148, 153, 155, 158, 172
Nutrition for the New Millennium – 17

O
Obesity – 110, 113
Occipital Lobe – 42
Oriental Medicine – 26
Orgone Energy – 27
Oscillatory Energy – 51

P
Paradigm – 15, 19, 21, 38, 40, 49, 52, 80, 112, 128-132, 140, 141
Parietal Lobe – 42
Particle Physics – 27, 51
Perfect Health – 21, 58, 73
Personal Resonance – 13, 22, 65
Petroleum Reserves – 176
Photon Energy – 27
Photoreceptor Cells – 135
Photosynthesis – 135, 170
Physics – 27, 51, 53
Pineal Gland – 38, 42, 67, 135, 136, 149, 150, 170, 171
Pinoline – 42, 43, 149, 150
Pituitary Gland – 31, 42, 150
Placebo Medicine – 61
Pnuema – 24, 160
Political Perspectives – 121
Politics – 8, 119-121, 151
Positive Planetary and Personal Progression – 112
Positive Thinking – 16, 58, 103, 146, 150
Poverty – 7, 15, 41, 111, 113, 119, 147, 148, 156
Prahlad Jani – 55, 109
Prana – See 'Chi'
Prana Protein Production – 175
Pranayama – 55, 70, 155, 157, 158, 160, 161, 163
Pranic Emissions – 52, 53
Pranic Flow – 7, 13-17, 19, 23, 28, 29, 31, 32, 37, 38, 40-43, 49, 52, 54, 55, 57-61, 68, 70, 71, 73, 75, 82, 86, 87, 90, 95, 96, 109, 110, 116, 117, 121, 127, 137, 144, 145, 149, 156158, 179
Pranic Force – 14, 15, 31
Pranic Healing – 24, 34, 108, 115, 159, 160
Pranic Nourishment – 14, 17, 31, 32, 59, 68-70, 96, 103, 109, 118, 121, 125, 127, 128, 132, 150, 153, 154, 156
Prayer – 43, 57, 65, 67, 71, 73, 112, 155
Pre-encodements – 102
Preparation Process – 58, 76
Preventative Medicine – 29, 86, 112, 114, 130
Presidents – 78, 119, 181
Programming – 38, 42, 45, 47, 58, 59, 61, 65, 68, 73, 74, 85, 88, 100, 106, 112, 148, 155, 163, 165
Proteins – 45
Pueblo Indians – 67
Purification – 31
Purity of Heart – 65, 66

Q
Qi – See 'Chi'
Qigong – 108, 111, 136, 137, 153, 155, 171
Quantum Electrodynamics – 27
Quantum Mechanics – 27, 51
Quantum Physics – 51, 53
Quantum Theory – 51

R
Rainforests – 175

Ram Bahadur Banjan – 55
Ramadan – 67
Recalibrate – 16, 42, 60, 72, 77
Reincarnation – 21, 52
Reiki – 34, 108, 116
Religion/s – 18, 19, 57, 115, 116, 121, 151
Religious Fervor – 42
Responsible Reporting – 129
Resonant Frequency – 51
Resource Redistribution – 24, 76, 118, 126, 141, 152, 172
Resource Sustainability – 113, 118, 174
Restoring Environmental Balance – 18
Retinohypothalamic Tract – 135
Reticular Formation – 40
Revelation – 42, 75
Rishis – 135
Romantic Love – 37
Ruah – 24, 160

S

Sadhus – 67
Safe Physical Conversion – 82
Scanning – 86, 87
Science of the Fields – 47, 56, 115, 179
Scientific Qigong Exploration – 137, 171
Scientific Testing – 52, 76
Scientific Law of Proportionality – 53
Self-help Therapy – 102
Self Love – 16, 37, 104, 110
Self Mastery – 40, 51, 61, 65, 105, 107, 120, 178
Self Refinement – 20
Sensitivity – 28, 38, 59, 96, 103, 114
Serapis Bay – 56
Service – 18, 20, 21, 39, 40, 47, 57, 61, 62, 65, 73, 79, 81, 85, 98, 111, 114, 129, 135, 140, 155, 156, 177
Seven Elements – 48, 165
Sewerage Systems – 176
Sexual Expression – 105
Shah, Dr Sudhir – See under 'D'
Shamans – 67, 128
Skepticism – 85, 128, 129
Sincerity – 65, 158
Social Interaction – 97, 99
Solar Nourishment – 28, 55, 108, 134, 140, 148, 169, 171, 173
Soul – 14, 21, 31, 67, 71, 135, 136, 161, 170
Soul's Evolution – 21
Sound Waves – 49, 50
Spectral Analysis – 37
Spiritual Anorexia – 24, 92, 196
Subatomic – 51
Super Conscious – 38
Superconductivity – 51
Superfluidity – 51
Supernatural – 14, 41
Suprachiasmatic Nucleus (SCN) – 135
Supreme Intelligence – 70
Surrender – 65, 92
Surya-Yoga – 70, 71, 96, 134

Suryanamaskar – 169
Sustenance – 21, 48, 92, 109
Synchronicity – 16, 19, 20, 115, 123
T
Taoist – 26, 35, 42, 55, 105
Tantra – 105
Tantric Sharing – 105
Telepathy / Telepathic – 39, 41, 49, 57, 83, 102, 106, 123
Temporal Lobe – 42
Tesla – 56
Terrorism – 18, 112, 156
Therovada School – 67
Theresa Nuemann – 172
Theta – 15, 16, 21, 32, 41, 42, 64 65, 92, 96, 103, 148, 158
Third Eye – 47, 135, 136, 170
Third World Aid – 7, 140
Third World Debt – 122, 178
Three Dimensional Freedom – 54
Tongue Positions – 42
Transcendental – 43
Two Dimensional Plane – 54
U
Underdeveloped Countries – 118
Unconditional Love – 28, 37, 97, 102, 105, 120
UNICEF – 153
Universal Field of Infinite Love and Intelligence (U.F.I) – 7, 24, 25, 38, 56, 57, 78, 79, 93, 106, 110, 124, 130, 131
Universal Law – 15, 39, 47, 50, 92, 111, 156, 178
Universal Law of Resonance – 39, 111
Universal Love – 43
Universal Mind – 14, 39, 69, 74, 87
Universal Paradigms – 38
Upanishads – 14, 157
Urination – 62
V
Vedic – 55, 64, 157, 159
Vegan – 92, 93, 98, 103, 124, 125
Vegetarian – 63, 65, 93, 98, 103, 109, 113, 118, 119, 124, 125, 128, 153, 174-176
Visualization – 43, 48, 146, 147, 149, 163, 168
Virtual Mass Space – 54
Vital Energy – 53
Vital Magnetism   27
Vitamins – 14, 32, 45, 59, 61, 63, 64, 85, 101, 150, 163, 166, 167
Violet Light – 38, 42, 45-49, 51, 54, 59, 89, 134, 149, 164, 166, 167
W
Weight Stabilization – 60
World Leaders – 78
World Peace – 177
Wiley Brooks – 55, 132
X
X-rays – 53, 172
Y
Yang – 26
Yin – 26
Yoga – 16, 55, 63, 69-71, 76, 87, 96, 102, 103, 108, 134, 136, 160, 163
Yom Kippur – 67

Z
Zen – 41
Zinaida Baranova – 55, 90, 109, 116
Other
21 Day Process – 55, 59, 72, 121, 123, 124, 126, 127, 130
5-MeO-DMT (5-methoxy-dimethyltryptamine) – 42, 43, 134, 149

THE PRANA PROGRAM
Enjoyable & Effective Evolution with Jasmuheen
e-book at http://www.selfempowermentacademy.com.au/htm/cia-education.asp#pranaprogram

JASMUHEEN'S BACKGROUND

- ♥ Author of 24 books;
- ♥ international lecturer,
- ♥ leading researcher on pranic nourishment;
- ♥ founder of the Self Empowerment Academy ;
- ♥ co-facilitator of the C.I.A. – the Cosmic Internet Academy; publisher and
- ♥ editor of the on-line M.A.P.S. Ambassadry Newsletter – *The ELRAANIS Voice (TEV)*.

- ❖ 1957 – Born in Australia to Norwegian immigrants
- ❖ 1959 – Began focus on vegetarianism
- ❖ 1964 – Began to study Chi
- ❖ 1971 – Discovered the Languages of Light
- ❖ 1974 – Initiated into Ancient Vedic Meditation and eastern philosophy
- ❖ 1974 – Began periodic fasting
- ❖ 1974 – Discovered telepathic abilities
- ❖ 1975 - 1992 – Raised children, studied and applied metaphysics, had various careers
- ❖ 1992 – Retired from corporate world to pursue metaphysical life
- ❖ 1992 – Met the Masters of Alchemy
- ❖ 1993 –Underwent Prana Initiation and began to live on light
- ❖ 1994 – Began 7 year research project on Divine Nutrition and pranic nourishment
- ❖ 1994 – Began global service agenda with the Ascended Masters
- ❖ 1994 – Received the first of 5 volumes of channelled messages from the Ascended Masters
- ❖ 1994 – Wrote *In Resonance*
- ❖ 1994 – Founded the Self Empowerment Academy in Australia
- ❖ 1994 – Began to hold classes in metaphysics and Self Mastery
- ❖ 1994 – Began *The Art of Resonance* newsletter renamed later as *The ELRAANIS Voice*
- ❖ 1995 – Traveled extensively around Australia, Asia and New Zealand sharing Self-Mastery research
- ❖ 1995 – Wrote *Pranic Nourishment (Living on Light) – Nutrition for the New Millennium*
- ❖ 1996 – Invited to present the Pranic Nourishment research to the Global stage
- ❖ 1996 – Began re-education program with the Global Media
- ❖ 1996 – Set up the International M.A.P.S. Ambassadry – Established in 33 countries
- ❖ 1996 – Created the C.I.A. – the Cosmic Internet Academy – a free website to download data for positive personal and planetary progression. Web address: www.selfempowermentacademy.com.au

THE PRANA PROGRAM
Enjoyable & Effective Evolution with Jasmuheen
e-book at http://www.selfempowermentacademy.com.au/htm/cia-education.asp#pranaprogram

- 1996 - 2001 – Traveled extensively to Europe, the U.K., the USA and Brazil with the 'Back to Paradise' agenda
- 1996 - 2004 – Talked about Divine Power and Divine Nutrition to > 900 million via the global media
- 1997 – Began to set up scientific research project for *Living on Light*
- 1997 – Began the Our Camelot Trilogy, wrote *The Game of Divine Alchemy*
- 1997 – Formed the M.A.P.S. Ambassadry Alliance – people committed to global harmony and peace
- 1998 – International tour to share the Impeccable Mastery Agenda
- 1998 – Wrote *Our Progeny – the X-Re-Generation*
- 1999 – Wrote the *Wizard's Tool Box* which later became the Biofields and Bliss Series.
- 1999 – Wrote *Dancing with my DOW : Media Mania, Mastery and Mirth*
- 1998 – 1999 Wrote and published *Ambassadors of Light – World Health World Hunger Project*
- 1999 – Began contacting World Governments regarding Hunger and Health Solutions
- 1999 – International tour to share the Blueprint for Paradise
- 1999 - 2001 – Began M.A.P.S. Ambassadors International Training Retreats
- 2000 – International tour 'Dancing with the Divine' to facilitate the election of an Etheric Government in 28 key cities and also shared the Luscious Lifestyles Program - L.L.P.
- 2000 - 2001 – Wrote *Cruising Into Paradise* an esoteric coffee table book
- 1999 - 2001 – Wrote *Divine Radiance – On the Road with the Masters of Magic* and
- 2001 – Wrote *Four Body Fitness : Biofields and Bliss Book 1*
- 2000 - 2001 – Launched the OPHOP agenda One People in Harmony on One Planet
- 2001 – Wrote the book *Co-Creating Paradise : Biofields and Bliss Book 2*
- 2001 – Launched Recipe 2000> as a tool to co-create global health and happiness; peace and prosperity for all on Earth
- 2002 – Launched www.jasmuheen.com with its Perfect Alignment Perfect Action Holistic Education Programs; and its I.R.S. focus to Instigate, Record and Summarize humanity's co-creation of paradise.
- 2002 – Did the 'Divine Radiance FOUR BODY FITNESS – Unity 2002' World Tour
- 2002 – Received, wrote and launched *The Madonna Frequency Planetary Peace Program* as the free e-book, *Biofields and Bliss Book 3*.
- 2002-2003 – Wrote *The Food of Gods*.
- 2003 – World Tour "Divine Nutrition and The Madonna Frequency Planetary Peace Project".
- 2004 – Wrote *The Law of Love* then toured with the Law of Love and Its Fabulous Frequency of Freedom agenda.
- 2005 – Wrote *Harmonious Healing and The Immortals Way*, then toured with the Harmonious Healing agenda.
- 2005 – Began work on *The Freedom of the Immortals Way* plus continued with writing *The Enchanted Kingdom Trilogy* & *The Prana Program* for Third World Countries.

THE PRANA PROGRAM
Enjoyable & Effective Evolution with Jasmuheen
e-book at http://www.selfempowermentacademy.com.au/htm/cia-education.asp#pranaprogram

---

- ❖ 2005 – Presented THE PRANA PROGRAM to the Society for Conscious Living at the United Nations Building in Vienna – Nov. 2005
- ❖ 2006 – International tour with THE PRANA PROGRAM

Jasmuheen's books are now published in 17 languages.

THE PRANA PROGRAM
Enjoyable & Effective Evolution with Jasmuheen
e-book at http://www.selfempowermentacademy.com.au/htm/cia-education.asp#pranaprogram

EDUCATIONAL E-BOOKS
http://www.selfempowermentacademy.com.au/htm/cia-education.asp

"IN RESONANCE": This book can be likened to a 'motor mechanic' manual except it is for tuning and aligning the four body system – physical, emotional, mental and spiritual – for a blissful life! The book covers 20 years of well-researched information on the Ancient Wisdom, plus many practical techniques to create positive change from breath and light work to bi-location, universal law, and telepathic communication! (No 2 with Esotera Magazine Best-seller – August 98 Germany) Add this e-book to shopping cart. http://payloadz.com/go?id=59295

THE DIVINE NUTRITION SERIES

BOOK 1 of the Living on Light – Divine Nutrition Series: "PRANIC NOURISHMENT – Nutrition for the New Millennium": Jasmuheen's fourth book which details her journey and experiences plus a detailed process, that allowed her to be physically sustained by the chi of life. This book also covers immortality and tools to stop the aging process. Living on Light is available in 15 languages – go to http://www.jasmuheen.com/who.asp#author for a list of publishers in other languages. Add this e-book to shopping cart http://payloadz.com/go?id=59292

BOOK 2 of the Living on Light – Divine Nutrition Series: "AMBASSADORS OF LIGHT – Living on Light – World Health, World Hunger Project" is Jasmuheen's tenth book and the follow on to her best seller *Pranic Nourishment – Nutrition for the New Millennium:* In this book Jasmuheen offers practical solutions to world health and world hunger related challenges. This entails an in-depth look at global disarmament, the dissolution of prohibition, the forgiveness of Third World debt, holistic re-education programs for long-term resource sustainability, and the elimination of all dis-ease. This book is a collation of research, recipes and recommendations that if adopted, will radically alter the path of humankind! Imagine a world without war or hunger or fear? Imagine a world that is dis-ease free and unified where all life is honored? These are the dreams of the Ambassadors of Light. Add this e-book to shopping cart http://payloadz.com/go?id=59293

BOOK 3 of the Living on Light – Divine Nutrition Series: "THE FOOD OF GODS": Powerful solutions, and meditations and tools on how to nourish all our hungers and eliminate our physical, emotional, mental and spiritual anorexia so that we can all be healthy and happy and peaceful and prosperous. Perfect nourishment utilizing Divine power. Jasmuheen's 18th book. Add this e-book to shopping cart http://payloadz.com/go?id=59294

"THE LAW OF LOVE": An extensive 238 A4 page manual filled with powerful life transforming meditations which also details the Ancient Taoist Masters techniques for Immortality plus Futuristic Science tools of Inter-Dimensional Matrix Mechanics for Jasmuheen's Freedom from Human Limitation Agenda. This research covers freedom from the need to age or create dis-ease; freedom from the to take food or liquid as we learn

THE PRANA PROGRAM
Enjoyable & Effective Evolution with Jasmuheen
e-book at http://www.selfempowermentacademy.com.au/htm/cia-education.asp#pranaprogram

---

how to create a self sustaining bio-system; freedom to express our Divine nature and all its gifts and glories … plus tested methods for determining our personal readiness levels for these freedoms! Add this e-book to shopping cart http://payloadz.com/go?id=91815 LAW OF LOVE: **Free Chapter:** http://www.selfempowermentacademy.com.au/htm/files/e-books-free/LAW-OF-LOVE-FREE-CHAPTER.pdf **Free Introduction & Chapter Titles** http://www.selfempowermentacademy.com.au/htm/files/e-books-free/LAW-OF-LOVE-INTRO-CHAPTER-TITLES.pdf

THE BIOFIELDS & BLISS TRILOGY:
BOOK 1: "FOUR BODY FITNESS": Written as a simple education manual for schools, in this book Jasmuheen shares details of Biofield Science which includes programming codes plus a lifestyle recipe that will create inner and outer peace; harmonize all people, and inspire great change. Bridging the ancient Wisdom with Futuristic Science, Biofields and Bliss also introduces the Higher Light Science of advanced bioenergetics and its pragmatic application for personal and global refinement. This book covers Recipe 2000> in great detail and offers many practical tools for successful living. Add this e-book to shopping cart http://payloadz.com/go?id=59243

BOOK 2: "CO-CREATING PARADISE": Covering the Dimensional Biofield Science of fine-tuning our Social and Global Biofields to create paradise on Earth, this book offers simple and powerful tools for positive personal & global transformation. It also provides a synopsis of religions, the ancient wisdom and quantum principles plus self-empowerment and peace tools. Add this e-book to shopping cart http://payloadz.com/go?id=59291

BOOK 3: "THE MADONNA FREQUENCY PLANETARY PEACE PROJECT": This free e-book carries the slogan "Change our Focus & Change our Future" and provides 9 practical projects and action plans and agreements and tuning tools that will create deep and lasting planetary peace by eliminating the root reasons and causes of war and terrorism. This manual is a timely, PERFECT ACTION solution for the chaos of this current millennium. Available ONLY as a free e-book. Also in **ENGLISH – DEUTSCH – ESPANOLE – FRANCAIS – ITALIANO – DUTCH – ROMANIAN – PORTUGUES – CZECHOSLOVAKIAN – CROATIAN.** http://www.selfempowermentacademy.com.au/htm/peace.asp

"DIVINE RADIANCE: ON THE ROAD WITH THE MASTERS OF MAGIC": A detailed account of the life of the messengers of the Masters of Magic. A 'heart' book filled with transformational tools and stories of Jasmuheen's interaction and experience with the ones she calls the Masters of Alchemy plus tips for improving our Divine Communication, Divine Revelations and more. Add this e-book to shopping cart http://payloadz.com/go?id=59297

THE PRANA PROGRAM
Enjoyable & Effective Evolution with Jasmuheen
e-book at http://www.selfempowermentacademy.com.au/htm/cia-education.asp#pranaprogram

---

"STREAMS OF CONSCIOUSNESS UNIFIED": A collection of recorded live channeling taken from the previous 5 volumes of the "Inspirations" trilogy and Vol. 1 and 2 of "Streams of Consciousness". As a volume of communications received by Jasmuheen from C.N.N., the Cosmic Nirvana Network, during the 1990's; these divinely inspired messages cover attitudes and life skills and as such will never date. Add this e-book to shopping cart http://payloadz.com/go?id=59301

JASMUHEEN'S meditations as MP3 files are now available at:
http://www.selfempowermentacademy.com.au/htm/cia-education.asp#audio

And in other languages at:
http://www.selfempowermentacademy.com.au/htm/cia-education.asp#audio-otherlanguage

Stay up to date with Jasmuheen's activities
via the Cosmic Internet Academy's Contact Updates List:
http://visitor.constantcontact.com/email.jsp?m=1011160294062
For those of you who choose to register with our C.I.A. CONTACT LIST,
you will receive general monthly or quarterly updates
or whenever we at the Self Empowerment Academy
and the C.I.A. feel there is something of value to share with you.

For more copies of this e-book go to:
http://www.selfempowermentacademy.com.au/htm/cia-education.asp

For more copies of this book go to:
www.lulu.com/content/395919

**Please note that your details are kept confidential at our C.I.A.
and are not passed on.**

THE PRANA PROGRAM
Enjoyable & Effective Evolution with Jasmuheen
e-book at http://www.selfempowermentacademy.com.au/htm/cia-education.asp#pranaprogram

THE PRANA PROGRAM
Enjoyable & Effective Evolution with Jasmuheen

Everything you need to know about prana.
Alternate Energy for the New Millennium,
including a practical Prana Program
for eliminating hunger in Third World countries.

Also The Prana Program presentation at
http://www.selfempowermentacademy.com.au/htm/divine.asp

Can we eliminate all health & hunger challenges on our planet?
Is there a way of satiating everyone's physical, emotional, mental and spiritual hungers and do it in a way that creates peace and harmony in our world?

After over a decade of experiential research in the field of alternate nourishment utilizing chi or prana – also known as cosmic particles – Jasmuheen as leading researcher in this field, now puts forth a program to do just that. Specializing in Third World countries, THE PRANA PROGRAM e-book is an encyclopedia type compendium of 'everything you always wanted to know about prana and more'. Styled in Question & Answer format this book covers alternate methods of nourishing and even hydrating the body using an inner energy source already produced in the body thus freeing us from our dependence on world's food resources and changing the economic status of our world.

Compiling questions from the last decade of her travels, this latest e-book also offers details on: Prana Program Benefits; Prana & the Bio-system; Prana & The Brain; Prana & Darkroom Technology; Prana & The Heart; Prana & The Cells; Prana & Field Science; Prana & Inter-dimensional Life; Preparation, Physical Changes & Preprogramming; Calibration, Testing & Comfortable Conversions; Social Scenes – Prana & Social Scenes; Prana & Parenting; Prana & Other Family Members – Harmonizing Households; Prana & eating Disorders; Prana & Sexuality; Global Issues – Gifts & Growth – Past, Present & Future; Prana & Health; Prana & Religion; The Prana Program & the Environment; The Prana Program & Politics; Skeptics & the Media; plus Solar Nourishment, Bigu & The Bigger Picture are in Chapters 2 to 8 of THE PRANA PROGRAM. Chapter 9 deals with a pragmatic simple nourishment system for both First and Third World health and hunger challenges.

ISBN 978-1-84728-343-6

O̲ Immortal̲ DOW̲
28   31   33 is

Death̲   Love̲
37   37 Match our
            Breathing
            to DOW